W9-AZG-971

Quik Notes

The Books
of the Bible

THE BOOKS
OF THE BIBLE

Philip W. Comfort, Ph.D.
Department of Biblical and Theological Studies
Wheaton College

James K. Hoffmeier, Ph.D.
Department of Bible, Theology, and Archeology
Wheaton College

with

C. Hassell Bullock, Ph.D.
Department of Bible, Theology, and Archeology
Wheaton College

Alfred J. Hoerth, M.A.
Department of Bible, Theology, and Archeology
Wheaton College

Edited by David P. Barrett

Tyndale House Publishers, Inc.
WHEATON, ILLINOIS

Visit Tyndale's exciting Web site at www.tyndale.com

Library of Congress Cataloging-in-Publication Data

Comfort, Philip Wesley.
  Quik notes on the books of the bible / Philip W. Comfort, James K. Hoffmeier, with
  C. Hassell Bullock, Alfred J. Hoerth ; editor, David P. Barrett.
    p. cm.
  Includes bibliographical references.
  ISBN 0-8423-5985-0 (pbk. : alk. paper)
  1. Bible—Introductions. I. Hoffmeier, James Karl, date II. Bullock, C. Hassell.
III. Hoerth, Alfred J. IV. Barrett, David P. V. Title.
BS475.2.C64 1999
220.6'1—dc20   95-40489

Printed in the United States of America

04 03 02 01 00 99
7   6   5   4   3   2   1

CONTENTS

Foreword

THE BIBLE is enjoyed throughout the world as literature, as history, and as Holy Scripture. Countless scholars have studied the Bible from various perspectives and interpretive frameworks, and countless others will no doubt carry on the endless scrutiny of Scripture.

It is important to note that the Bible can indeed be understood from each of the three perspectives mentioned above (literature, history, and Holy Scripture) without necessarily compromising the integrity of the other two perspectives. While many scholars reject the Bible's claim to be a written account of God's revelation to humanity, this view of Scripture does not automatically exempt these scholars from allowing personal biases to influence their conclusions regarding the Bible, nor does it necessarily amplify this tendency. The truth is, pure objectivity is impossible to achieve. Reason and scholarly method can be employed with equal vigor by those who hold the Bible to be Holy Scripture and by those who do not hold this view.

The writers of this work were educated in biblical and Near Eastern studies at institutions that generally do not treat the biblical text as divinely inspired. As a result, they are aware of the most significant criticisms leveled against the Bible and of the most credible responses to these criticisms. While the writers acknowledge that some portions of Scripture were never intended to be interpreted literally or historically, nevertheless they hope to communicate to the reader that the Bible is a coherent document, that the characters portrayed were real people, and that God is truly revealed through the messages given to human agents and through his actions in history.

The goal of this book is to give readers an overview of the content and context of the books of the Holy Bible. The summaries included in this work highlight major themes in each of the books and draw attention to such features as style, viewpoints, and emphases of each biblical writer. By developing a better understanding of the content and context of each book, readers will be better equipped to grasp the larger message of the Bible and the beliefs of Judaism and of the early Christian church.

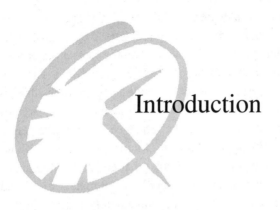

Introduction

The Old Testament, or the Hebrew Bible, is a collection of books (usually referred to as a canon) that was compiled over several hundreds of years before the birth of Jesus Christ (ca. 1400–400 B.C.). Sacred to Christians and revered in the Koran, the Old Testament is, first and foremost, the religious, sociological, and historical book of the Jewish people. In the Hebrew manuscript tradition, the Old Testament is divided into three canonical units: the Law (*Torah*), the Prophets (*Nebiim*), and the Writings (*Kethubim*). Hence the acronym *TANAKH,* the Jewish term for the Old Testament. These units are comprised of the following books:

Law—Genesis, Exodus, Leviticus, Numbers, and
   Deuteronomy
Prophets—Joshua, Judges, 1 and 2 Samuel, 1 and 2 Kings,
   Isaiah, Jeremiah, Ezekiel, and the twelve minor prophets
Writings—Psalms, Proverbs, Job, Song of Songs, Ruth,
   Lamentations, Ecclesiastes, Esther, Daniel, Ezra,
   Nehemiah, and 1 and 2 Chronicles

Many readers today are unfamiliar with this arrangement of books. The sequence most widely recognized by English Bible readers reflects the order established by the translators of the Septuagint, a Greek translation of the Hebrew Bible. The Septuagint was assembled in Alexandria, Egypt, in the third century B.C. Using a more Hellenistic approach to literary organization, the translators arranged the sequence according to genre: Law, History, Poetry and Wisdom, Major Prophets, and Minor Prophets. As a result, several books changed categories, such as Daniel, which was moved to the Major Prophets, and 1 and 2 Chronicles, which were placed immediately after 2 Kings.

Jewish literature does not contain any records regarding how the Old Testament received its final form, how it received its three-part structure, or why certain books were included and others omitted. The earliest reference to the present Jewish arrangement is recorded in the introduction to the book of Ecclesiasticus (a noncanonical work). In 132 B.C., the grandson of the author, Jesus Ben Sirach, translated the work into Greek. He penned these words in the foreword: "The knowledge of many great things has been given to us through the Law, the Prophets, and the other books that followed them." By that time a formal title for the third section had not been established. Around A.D. 30, Jesus Christ referred to the Hebrew canon as "the law of Moses, the prophets, and the psalms" (Luke 24:44, NRSV). Psalms, it should be noted, stands as the first book in the Writings section, and thus he was most likely referring to the entire corpus of the Writings, rather than just the book of Psalms.

It is not certain when the books within the three units were accepted in the Jewish community as authoritative or scriptural. Before the discovery of the now famous Dead Sea Scrolls, it was thought by some that the Law received its canonical form by 400 B.C., the Prophets by 200 B.C., and the Writings at the Council of Jamnia (Jabneh) in A.D. 90. But this view was drastically altered in 1948 when the scrolls, some of which date to the second century B.C., were discovered. The fact that much of the Septuagint was translated around 250 B.C. should alert scholars to an earlier date for the closing of the Old Testament canon.

A council of rabbis met in Jamnia, Palestine, in A.D 90 and endorsed the three-part canon, not so much making it authoritative for the first time, but sending a clear message to the Jewish community that any new Christian (New Testament) books were most definitely not part of the Hebrew canon. The Council of Jamnia simply reaffirmed a commitment to the received canon.

The Law was clearly viewed as Scripture by the Hebrew prophets, who cite it as the basis for their message. The prophets sought to turn the people back to the covenant stipulations set forth in the Law. The date range on prophetic literature for both major and minor prophets spans from the eighth to the fifth centuries. The books of the Writings display the widest range of dates, with the Psalms from the tenth century B.C. and the later postexilic books from the fifth century B.C.

Thus the earliest possible date for the canonizing of the entire corpus of Old Testament books would be sometime during the fifth century B.C. A Jewish tradition from about 100 B.C. credits Nehemiah (fifth century B.C.) with assembling the various collections into a library that included "books about the kings and the prophets, [and] the writings of David" (2 Maccabees 2:13). While the closing of the Hebrew canon could have taken place as early as Nehemiah, it is also likely that the canon was closed a century later.

. . . . .APOCRYPHA

Readers of the *New Jerusalem Bible* or the Common Bible edition of the *New Revised Standard Version* will be aware of a number of books that are not found in other translations of the Bible. The books of 1 and 2 Maccabees, Tobit, Judith, and Ben Sirach (or Ecclesiasticus) are among the thirteen works commonly referred to as the Apocrypha. Written mostly during the second through first centuries B.C., these books consist primarily of histories, short stories, wisdom literature, and additions to canonical books. Apparently many Jews of the second century A.D. did not consider these books to be Scripture, insisting that prophecy began with Moses and ended with Ezra (ca. 440 B.C.). Jesus Ben Sirach added a disclaimer in the foreword to his own book, Ecclesiasticus, so that it would not be mistaken for Scripture. He writes that he had studied the Scriptures and wrote Ecclesiasticus to help the reader "make progress in living according to the law of Moses." The books of the Apocrypha were not recognized by the Council of Jamnia, nor by the New Testament writers, nor by the Christian church fathers. They were found in early Greek Bibles originating in Egypt but not in Hebrew versions of the Old Testament. As he translated the Latin Vulgate, Jerome reluctantly included these extra books, calling them "apocryphal." During the Protestant Reformation, Luther and others rejected these books, claiming that they were not divinely inspired.

At the Council of Trent in A.D. 1546, perhaps as a reaction to the Reformers' rejection of the Apocrypha, the Roman Catholic Church declared the books of the Apocrypha to be inspired and therefore Scripture. Despite the exclusion of these books from the Protestant canon, the Apocrypha is a major source for studying the development of Judaism during the period between the Old and New Testaments. Careful and critical investigation of this corpus of literature is imperative for understanding the religious, social, theological, and historical background of the New Testament.

NEW TESTAMENT

The New Testament is made up of twenty-seven books written by Christians during the first century. Many of these "books" are actually letters written to churches that needed instruction or correction in their understanding and practice of Christianity.

Other books, such as the four Gospels and Acts, detail the life and actions of significant figures in early Christianity. Still others, such as the book of Revelation, were written to encourage believers in their Christian faith. One feature held in common by all the books, however, is the foundational belief that Jesus Christ is the Messiah, the one sent to redeem humanity from the evil one. It is also important to note that the New Testament books were written to believers and are often difficult to understand unless they are approached from this perspective.

After the various books of the New Testament were written and began circulating among the churches, Christians collected certain books into volumes. In the first century, each of the four Gospels was treated as an individual book about Jesus' life and ministry. By the late second century, Christians had collected the four Gospels into one volume. Paul's epistles were also collected into a single volume—perhaps as early as the end of the first century. Later, in the second and third centuries, Acts and the General Epistles were combined into one volume.

In the first century, the Hebrew Bible (later renamed the "Old Testament" by Christians) was considered the Bible for Christians as well. It seemed only natural to include the Hebrew Bible in the canon of Christian books, since many Christian beliefs find their roots in Judaism. Christians read the Old Testament and taught from it in their meetings. They also had the testimonies of the apostles who were among them. The apostles instructed the churches and passed on to them the teachings of Jesus. But after the apostles died, Christians were dependent upon what the apostles had written regarding Jesus Christ. At the same time, they began to recognize the apostles' writings as authoritative in the same way they regarded the Old Testament as Scripture. Several New Testament books were regarded as inspired Scripture as early as the second century.

Before a book could be included in the New Testament canon

of Scripture, it had to measure up to a threefold standard: (1) It had to be authored by an apostle, by an associate of an apostle, or by a relative of Jesus (i.e., James or Jude); (2) it had to contain spiritual truths that could be taught as Christian doctrine; and (3) it had to be regarded by successive generations of Christians as being edifying, enlightening, and inspiring.

By the end of the first century, the New Testament canon included the four Gospels, Acts, Paul's epistles, 1 Peter, and 1 John. Other books took longer to gain acceptance into the canon of Christian writings: Hebrews (because the author was unknown), James (because it was thought to have doctrinal differences with Paul's theology on salvation), 2 Peter and Jude (because their authorship was in question), 2 and 3 John (because they were fairly unknown), and Revelation (because its message and authorship were debated). By the fourth century, most of the issues hindering canonization were resolved, and the twenty-seven books that now comprise the New Testament were recognized by the church as authoritative.

In the final arrangement of the New Testament books, the Gospels come first, recounting the life and actions of Jesus and his disciples. The early church regarded Matthew as the first gospel to have been written, and the genealogy that opens this Gospel provides a logical link between the Old Testament and the New Testament. Mark was thought to have been written next, followed by Luke and Acts. It seemed logical to place John's Gospel among the other Gospels, and so Acts comes after John in canonical order. The letters of Paul are next, arranged according to size rather than order of composition. Likewise, the other letters that follow Paul's are arranged by size as well. Revelation appropriately concludes the New Testament with its prophetic warnings and promises of future restoration.

Historical Overview

. . . . .THE PATRIARCHAL PERIOD—ISRAEL'S ORIGINS

The Old Testament could very well be described as the history of a family, the father of which was Abraham. **Genesis** 1–11 traces the prehistory of the family back to Shem, the son of Noah, and then even farther back to Adam. The main characters, Abraham, Isaac, Jacob, and Joseph, then take center stage beginning at Genesis 12. From chapter 12 onward, these forefathers of the nation of Israel remain the central focus of Genesis.

Critical scholarship has proposed varying opinions as to the historicity of these figures. At the beginning of the twentieth century the patriarchs were considered no more than manufactured roots to help give identity to a dispersed Jewish nation. Later archaeological recovery of Near Eastern history has since resulted in a heightened respect for the patriarchal narratives in Genesis. Recently, however, but without the benefit of new data, there have been renewed attempts to revive the earlier extreme position.

The patriarchs are not mentioned by name in any ancient Near Eastern text, but their lifestyles fit nicely within the time period assigned them in the Bible. It would be highly unlikely that the parallels could be so strong if the patriarchs were indeed an invention of late first-millennium B.C. writers. The character of **Job** also reflects much of the lifestyle of this period, although it is uncertain when this book was written.

Abraham

Abraham was born in approximately 2000 B.C. By this time the Near East had already passed through millennia of physical and social development. The famed pyramids of Egypt were already several centuries old, and Mesopotamia had long since codified law. The patriarchs, therefore, were not primitive men. They functioned in highly complex societies, and their lives were filled with countless chores as they attended to life's necessities. Humanity has progressed little more than technologically since the time of the patriarchs.

Abraham's life can be divided into three phases: his years at Ur, his period of mobility, and his life in Canaan. The Bible glosses over the first of these phases, specifying only that he lived in a city named Ur in southern Mesopotamia ("Ur of the Chaldeans"). Occasional attempts to place his birth in northwestern Mesopotamia have little merit and would require emending more than a few simple verses in Genesis. Extrabiblically, much is known about this southern city of Ur, and it appears that Abram lived in a very sophisticated society. Politically, however, if Abram was born shortly after 2000 B.C., he would have found himself in a turbulent setting as the once-proud city of Ur was buffeted by a series of contending powers.

It could have been this political uncertainty in southern Mesopotamia that led Abram's polytheistic father to take his extended family northwest to the city of Haran, where, as at Ur, the moon god was the primary deity. The Bible is silent as to what effect the father's polytheism had on his son Abram. One can only speculate on Abram's early religious convictions.

While Abram was at Haran, God made a promise to him, vowing to raise up a great nation from his descendants. In response to this promise, Abram obediently moved south into Palestine. He did not journey alone or empty-handed. In fact, he entered Palestine as a rich man, commanding a large operation of workers and livestock. No doubt due to Palestine's bustling population, Abram continued southward to the Negev to find an open area for his entourage.

Famine apparently hit Palestine shortly after Abram's arrival, and so he migrated west into Egypt, along with many others at this time. According to the chronological framework provided by Genesis, Egypt was then in its Twelfth Dynasty (1963–1789 B.C.), a prosperous and confident time when Egyptians would have monitored, but allowed, such movements into their eastern delta region. In Egypt, Abram's fear for his personal safety led him into deception, difficulty, and eventual expulsion. Pharaoh's attraction to Abram's wife could have been motivated by a wish to promote commercial interests between Egypt and Palestine, as much as by physical desire.

Abram's return to Bethel in Palestine marks the end of his period of mobility and the beginning of the final phase of his life. The Bible records the difficulties encountered by Abram's nephew Lot and the need for Abraham to rescue his relative from a raiding party. At this time Abram's name was changed to Abraham, meaning "father of many," and God's covenant promise would be echoed each time Abraham's name was mentioned. The interaction between Abraham and his nephew gives insight into the character of Abraham and of the rest of society at that time.

During this period the cities of Sodom and Gomorrah were destroyed for their wickedness. The means by which God chose to destroy the two cities is open to different interpretations. Traditionally, the cities have been thought to be submerged under the south end of the Dead Sea. Recent attempts to locate the cities elsewhere require a drastic time shift in the biblical story.

Extrabiblical texts like the Nuzi tablets found in northeast Iraq early in the twentieth century have greatly increased our ability to understand patriarchal thoughts and actions. The Bible clearly shows the anguish Abraham felt over his lack of an heir, but the reason for his anguish is made even clearer when the purpose of marriage and children is seen from a second-millennium B.C. vantage point. For example, childless couples might adopt a son to ensure that the family name would continue and that they would be cared for in their later years. In exchange for this form of old-age insurance, the adopted son was made the heir.

It may be that Abraham had established this type of adoptive relationship with Eliezer in order to ensure the existence of an heir. In any case, it is clear that Abraham agreed to his wife's plea that they try another option commonly practiced in that day. A barren wife could be, and sometimes was, required to provide her husband with a fertile woman. Ishmael was subsequently born of Sarah's handmaiden, and Abraham assumed that this son would be the heir to his wealth and to the covenant promise from God. The later birth of Isaac to Sarah corrected this view, and the near-sacrifice of Isaac can be viewed as a final sealing of the covenant between God and Abraham. It was clear that Abraham was willing to give everything he had in order to obey God.

Sarah died shortly thereafter, and Abraham buried her in a cave bought either from Hittites living far from their homeland, or from Hethites, an otherwise unknown local Canaanite subgroup. Abraham remarried and had additional children. In time he was buried beside Sarah.

Although the covenant promise began to be fulfilled in Isaac's birth, all Abraham ever personally owned of the Promised Land was the cave and adjoining field where he buried Sarah. But

Abraham died still believing the covenant would come to fruition.

Isaac

As with Abraham, the Bible recounts the events of Isaac's life from birth to death. The most famous episode in Isaac's early years was his brush with death as his father displayed his total allegiance to God by offering Isaac as a burnt offering. Isaac's own reaction to this incident can only be imagined.

In keeping with the societal norms of the day, Isaac entered into an arranged marriage with Rebekah. Again, however, there arose the problem of infertility. Isaac must have been frustrated by his inability to fulfill the covenant that promised vast numbers of descendents from Abraham's line. But Isaac did not try to take matters into his own hands as his father had done. Instead, Isaac prayed for divine help, and soon he was the father of twin boys, Jacob and Esau.

Before the birth of his sons, Isaac did imitate his father in one instance. At Gerar Isaac passed Rebekah off to the Philistines as his sister. As with Abraham in both Egypt and Gerar, Isaac was found out and rebuked. This interaction with the Philistines is seen by some as an anachronism, since the Philistines did not reach Palestine in large numbers until centuries later. The possibility also exists, however, that an early group of Sea Peoples, to whom the Philistines belonged, had settled in this part of Palestine.

At Gerar Isaac demonstrated his peaceful disposition. The envy generated by Isaac's material success caused him to relocate more than once rather than to stay and fight. Isaac's identification with God was so strong, however, that his neighbors did not want to provoke him too much.

The remainder of Isaac's life revolved around the actions of his sons, by whom he found himself both tricked and manipulated. Such negative portraits of significant figures make biblical history different from records preserved elsewhere in the Near East. Extrabiblical records rarely admit to faults and failings in their heros. This is not so in the Bible, where the shortcomings of biblical characters are evident and help make their lives believable. Isaac had fears and faults, but he also exhibited closeness and dependence upon God, faithfulness to his father, and love for his wife. Isaac's life formed a necessary link in the covenant promise of God.

Jacob

The Bible skips over the formative years of Jacob and Esau and simply notes that they developed personalities that were quite different from each other. The first significant event noted about these twins occurred when Esau sold his birthright to his younger brother in exchange for a meal. Every male child was entitled to inherit a share of his father's estate, but the birthright of the eldest son entitled him to the family name and prestige and to a double portion of his father's wealth. There is at least one extrabiblical parallel (a Nuzi contractual document) to this seemingly disparate exchange, but the motives of the two brothers are still uncertain. Perhaps Esau thought that no one would ever believe he had been foolish enough to agree to such a transfer. There is no mention that Jacob ever used the event to claim his inheritance.

Jacob and Esau are not mentioned again until they reach middle-age. Then the favoritism shown earlier by their parents surfaced once more when Isaac made plans to bless Esau.

Rebekah laid plans to ensure that the blessing would go to her favorite son, Jacob. Through the senses of smell, touch, and taste the aged Isaac was betrayed into thinking that the disguised and lying Jacob was really Esau. Esau appeared shortly after Isaac had finished blessing Jacob, but by then it was not possible to negate the blessing. In ancient societies, great weight was attached to the spoken word, and God would have been regarded as a witness in such a blessing. There was little Isaac could do for his favorite son.

It became clear to Rebekah, however, that Jacob had to escape his brother's wrath. She convinced Isaac it was time for Jacob to visit relatives in the north in order to find a wife. As he journeyed northward, Jacob had a dream in which he saw a stairway connecting heaven and earth. In this dream, Jacob personally heard the covenant promise from God for the first time. In that communication God assured Jacob that he would not forsake him.

Jacob then joined his uncle Laban's family. Since he lacked the bride price for Rachel, the daughter of his choice, Jacob contracted to work for his uncle for a number of years. At the end of the set period, Jacob was tricked into marrying Rachel's older sister, Leah. When Jacob furiously approached his uncle after the deception was discovered, Laban explained that he had only followed local marriage custom. Nevertheless, he placated Jacob by suggesting that he continue with the wedding celebration, and then afterward he would also be given Rachel as his wife. Jacob agreed, and so he began the week as a bachelor and ended it as the husband of two wives.

Jacob preferred Rachel to her sister, Leah, but it was Leah who first bore sons for Jacob. From the names she gave the boys, Reuben ("Look, a son!") and Simeon ("one who hears"), it is clear that Leah hoped their births would encourage Jacob to love her more. By the time the fourth son was born, however, Leah was resigned to her fate. Rachel responded to these births by providing her handmaiden to Jacob, and sons were born to her credit by this means. Leah then did the same with her handmaiden, and it was only after the birth of ten sons and one daughter that Rachel finally bore a child of her own, Joseph.

By this time Jacob felt it was time to return home, but his

uncle convinced him to stay because he had been blessed by Jacob's presence. A new work arrangement was agreed upon by the two men, but Laban repeatedly broke the agreement. Jacob then devised a scheme to get back at his uncle. The ensuing episode of the stripped poles at the watering troughs has puzzled commentators. One explanation is that Jacob was tricking his uncle into thinking that he was achieving his success through magic, when, in fact, he was engaging in selective breeding.

Twenty years after Jacob left home, God instructed him to return. Jacob probably reasoned that his father-in-law would refuse him permission to leave, so he secretly moved his family and wealth southward. Laban pursued Jacob but did not catch up with him until he was near the north end of the Jordan River. Laban was angry because he was unable to find the god statues Rachel had stolen. It is difficult to be certain whether Rachel hoped to later use the god statues to claim part of her father's wealth, or whether she held a religious attachment to the statues and used them for protection in her travels. The two men then established a nonaggression pact, and Laban placed a potential curse on Jacob should the pact ever be broken.

Although free from Laban, Jacob soon felt another danger. His brother, Esau, was approaching from the south with four hundred men. Jacob prayed for protection and tried to appease Esau by sending hundreds of animals as presents. The night before the brothers were reunited, Jacob became entangled in a wrestling match with a stranger. When Jacob prevailed, the man blessed him and renamed him Israel, meaning "one who struggles with God."

The meeting of the brothers proved peaceful, and soon Esau headed back south. Jacob moved west, first to Succoth and then across the Jordan to Shechem. Tragically, Jacob's daughter Dinah was raped there, and her brothers took revenge by killing every male and plundering the city. Following this debacle, God told Jacob to move to Bethel, where he then repeated his blessing on Jacob. While traveling from Bethel to Bethlehem, Rachel's wish for a second child was realized at the expense of her life. Benjamin was born.

Joseph

Joseph is the last main character in the book of Genesis. Born in Haran, he was the first son of Rachel and the most favored son of Jacob. No insights are recorded about Joseph's life, however, until he was seventeen years old. By this time, tension had been mounting between Joseph and his brothers as a result of Jacob's obvious preference for Joseph and of Joseph's own dreams of future superiority over his brothers.

Despite the sibling friction, Joseph was sent one day to check on his brothers, who were tending sheep many miles away. Joseph's arrival in his specially made coat caused his brothers' hatred to boil over, and so they threw him into a pit. Later they sold him as a slave to a caravan en route to Egypt and led Jacob to think that Joseph had been killed by a wild animal.

Joseph entered an Egypt that was different in several ways from the land Abraham had known. During the intervening time, the Middle Kingdom had faltered and had been taken over by foreigners whom the Egyptians called Hyksos. It is now generally accepted that the Hyksos originated in Palestine. Whatever the case, Egypt was a free and confident country in Abraham's day, but it had become an occupied country by the time Joseph arrived. In spite of this difference, however, Egypt may have appeared much the same in many ways, since the Hyksos assumed the veneer of the classic Egyptian lifestyle. They used the same titles for kingship as the Egyptians had used, and some even adopted Egyptian names, writing their inscriptions in hieroglyphics. Some collected Egyptian literature. Many adopted the Egyptian gods Set and Re as their own. Though they were not ethnic Egyptians, the Hyksos imitated much of Egyptian culture while maintaining some Syro-Canaanite traditions.

Joseph was sold to Potiphar, the captain of Pharaoh's body-guard, and was put to work in his house. Joseph's work attracted Potiphar's attention, and he was promoted to overseer of the house, a supervisory position in the estates of Egyptian royalty. While attending to his duties as overseer, Joseph was often watched by Potiphar's wife, who eventually tried to seduce the young slave. Joseph refused the advances of Potiphar's wife but was thrown into prison on a trumped-up charge of attempted rape.

In prison Joseph encountered two fellow inmates who had worked for Pharaoh. One night these two men had dreams that greatly troubled them, and they wanted the dreams to be interpreted for them. Throughout the Near East, dreams were thought to be a form of "god talk." That is, dreams were one way the gods told people what they should do or what was going to happen in the future. There were even dream interpretation manuals that would help concerned dreamers figure out what certain dreams meant. The two officials desired to know specifically what their dreams meant, and they probably did not have access to such manuals in prison. Joseph the dream teller became the dream interpreter, and within three days his interpretations proved correct.

Eventually Pharaoh also became troubled by some dreams, but neither his wise men nor his magicians could supply a satisfactory interpretation. Joseph was called before Pharaoh, but before he answered Pharaoh's questions, he declared God to be the one who gives true interpretations. Joseph then gave his interpretation, which predicted an impending famine, and offered a plausible solution for surviving it. Pharaoh was so impressed that he appointed Joseph to oversee preparations for the lean years.

Joseph's sudden rise in station must be seen in the context of its time. First, Egypt was still ruled by the Hyksos, who were foreigners with a Semitic background similar to Joseph's. Second, the religious importance attached to dreams made it logical to elevate someone who had demonstrated ability in reading the minds of the gods. Finally, Egypt always lived with a fear that the next year's flooding of the Nile might be disastrous. A couple of feet too little of inundation meant that, no matter how well the water was utilized, the following harvest would be lean. Conversely, if the Nile overflowed its banks a couple of feet too much, the dikes and low-lying villages would be wiped out and the harvest would again be adversely affected.

Joseph's preparations for the expected famine years were so successful that attempts to tabulate the stored supplies were finally suspended. When the predicted lean years began, Palestine was affected as well as Egypt. This famine in Palestine forced Jacob to send all his sons except Benjamin, his only remaining link with Rachel, into Egypt to buy grain. In Egypt the brothers had to approach the overseer, Joseph, before buying grain.

As his brothers bowed before him, Joseph began to see the fruition of his own dreams. Joseph recognized his brothers, but they did not recognize him, almost certainly because of his young age when sold into slavery and his new Egyptian appearance.

Joseph supplied his family with grain but placed Simeon in jail in order to coerce his brothers to return with Benjamin. After the food supply was depleted, Jacob allowed Benjamin to accompany the other brothers on a second trip to Egypt. This time, after playing more cat-and-mouse games, Joseph revealed himself to his brothers, assuring them that he had forgiven them and would not seek revenge. The brothers then hurried back home and told their father that Joseph was still alive.

Shortly thereafter Jacob led his extended family into Egypt to settle in Goshen, the eastern portion of the Nile delta. Jacob and Joseph eventually died in Egypt, and both were mummified. Joseph's age at death is not entirely certain because 110 years was an Egyptian expression used simply to indicate that someone had lived to a ripe old age.

As Jacob and his extended family left Palestine and entered Goshen, the patriarchal period came to a close, and the period of the Egyptian sojourn began.

▸ . . . . THE EGYPTIAN SOJOURN AND THE EXODUS

The Oppression and Deliverance of Israel

The time interval between the end of Genesis (the death of Joseph) and the beginning of **Exodus** is not stated. Life in Egypt for the Hebrews had been favorable for some time, but after several generations a significant change occurred. The new king did not know of Joseph, which implies that a new dynasty had come to power. The paranoia expressed by this unnamed king over the large number of Hebrews in the northeastern delta of Egypt seems to reflect a concern with the security of his country's northern border. Pharaoh Ahmose had driven out the hated Hyksos and founded the Eighteenth Dynasty (1550–1300 B.C.). If he is the king mentioned in the book of Exodus, then his fears about a possible invasion or uprising and about the large numbers of Israelites living in Goshen fits the situation well.

In order to maintain tight control over his resident aliens, the king of Egypt conscripted Hebrews to work on Egyptian building projects such as the store cities of Pithom and Raamses. Both Eighteenth- and Nineteenth-Dynasty pictorial and textual evidence depicts the forced labor of prisoners and resident aliens and provides a sense of the toil involved in such construction projects.

As the population of the Hebrews grew, tensions between the

Egyptians and the Hebrews mounted. Finally the king of Egypt imposed a policy of partial genocide to hold down the foreign population. It was during this dangerous period that Moses was born. In order to save her only son from infanticide, Moses' mother placed her child in a basket and set him afloat on the Nile River. Moses was then found and spared by Pharaoh's daughter, and his mother was selected to raise him in the royal household. Moses was reared as an Egyptian and thoroughly educated in the Egyptian language, literature, and religion. The training of Moses is reflective of the Eighteenth Dynasty practice of taking foreign Palestinian princes hostage in Egypt to ensure the loyalty of their fathers. The Egyptians acculturated these princes for possible future use as puppets in their native kingdoms.

Despite his Egyptian upbringing, Moses maintained his Hebrew identity, and this caused him to intercede for another Hebrew and kill an Egyptian. As a result, Moses had to flee the country for his life. He relocated in Midian, east of the Sinai Peninsula, where he stayed for a number of years with a priest named Jethro. Eventually he married one of Jethro's daughters. Years later, while tending sheep in the area of Mount Sinai, Moses had an encounter with God through a burning bush. He was told to return to Egypt to be God's spokesperson before Pharaoh. Moses reluctantly returned to his homeland.

In Egypt Moses approached Pharaoh and requested time off for the Hebrews in order that they might worship their God in the desert. Pharaoh refused, perhaps taking this request as an affront to the Egyptian notion that the king was himself a god, the son of the sun god Re. Instead of granting the Hebrews time off, Pharaoh increased their workload. Pharaoh's stubbornness eventually precipitated a series of ten plagues from the God of the Hebrews.

The plagues, frequently called the "signs and wonders" in the Old Testament, could have been understood by the Egyptians as attacks against their own gods and by the Hebrews as evidences that their God controlled nature. The tenth plague, the death of every firstborn male, was different from the previous nine plagues because the Israelites would also be affected. They had to make special preparations to avoid the loss of their own eldest sons. The Hebrews called this event Passover, and their descendants still remember and observe this deliverance every year.

The death of every firstborn son, including the crown prince, temporarily convinced the intransigent Pharaoh to allow the Hebrews to leave Egypt. The traditional translation of the numbers of Hebrews who left Egypt with Moses often results in a total of between 2 and 3 million people when women and children are added to the Bible's census of fighting men. Such a total seems excessively high in light of Egypt's probable total population. The logistical problems such a number would have encountered in Sinai also calls the traditional translation into question. Since the key Hebrew word *elef* not only means "thousand," but also carries the sense of "clan" or "military unit," it is possible that the numbers involved in the Exodus and in the conquest of Canaan were considerably less than millions, perhaps only as many as thirty thousand.

Despite occasional claims to the contrary, as of yet there is no Egyptian record of the Hebrews' Egyptian sojourn, nor of the Exodus. This silence is, however, understandable if we assume that Joseph functioned within the Hyksos period. When the Hyksos were overthrown, the Egyptians made a concerted effort to erase from history any record of the foreigners' domination. The Egyptians were so successful that Egyptologists have difficulty reconstructing the Hyksos period. Any record of Joseph could have been lost in that purge. Concerning the Exodus, the Egyptians were seldom interested in writing about those they considered nonpeoples and were extremely reluctant to record setbacks. It is possible that no record of this portion of history would have ever been made.

The Journey to Mount Sinai and the Sinaitic Covenant

Immediately after the tenth plague fell upon every unmarked home in Egypt, the Hebrews left Egypt in what has since been called the Exodus. The exact route of the Exodus is uncertain. Scholarly discussion centers upon the location of the sea that the Hebrews crossed in order to escape the pursuing Egyptian army. The Hebrew phrase for this body of water is simply "the sea" or the "sea of reeds." The Septuagint translation renders the same word as "Red Sea." The "sea of reeds" could refer to one of the several sizeable lakes on the eastern side of the delta, such as Lake Timsah or the Bitter Lakes. Exactly where the crossing took place is unknown, but the divine rescue and the destruction of Pharaoh's army was, and is, so important to Israel's concept of God's saving acts that it would be difficult to dismiss it as a fabrication by later biblical writers.

With the Egyptians safely out of the picture, Moses led the Hebrews (hereafter called "the Israelites") to Mount Sinai, the place where he had earlier received instructions from God. Several proposals have been made for the exact identification of this mountain, but a location in southern Sinai is most likely. Along the way the Israelites encountered thirst, hunger, and armed conflict. Throughout the three months' journey, God visibly led, fed, and protected his people.

Moses' purpose for leading the Israelites to Mount Sinai was to introduce the nation to their God, who had miraculously delivered them from Egypt. When the Israelites reached Mount Sinai, they observed a period of preparation and consecration before they were ready to meet God. This moment was a critical turning point in the history of Israel. God was going to make a covenant, or treaty, with the nation of Israel. The covenant would resemble a marriage contract between a groom and his bride. This new covenant defined God's relationship to the Israelites, the Israelites' relationship to God, the moral and social code that would set them apart as belonging to God, and the ceremonial code to be followed by the priesthood. The Decalogue, or Ten Commandments, formed the core of this new treaty. These were written on stone tablets by God himself and were given to Moses to be presented to the new nation of Israel. The book of **Leviticus** largely records Moses' instructions from God concerning the priesthood and matters related to holiness and purity.

Israel's Apostasy and Moses' Intercession
While Moses was on the mountain receiving further instructions from God, the people of Israel became restless. Thinking that Moses had abandoned them on Mount Sinai, they wanted to move on from the inhospitable environs of the area. They pressed their priest, Aaron, the older brother of Moses, to make them an image to lead them to their promised homeland. The people fashioned a golden calf or young bull and proclaimed that this god had delivered them from Egypt. God was infuriated by this act of direct disobedience to the newly established covenant, and Moses dashed the tablets of the covenant to the ground. Moses might have been trying to nullify the treaty, thereby keeping the curses of the covenant from overtaking Israel. Regardless, God threatened to destroy the disobedient Israelites, but Moses interceded for them. After Moses' prayer, God decided not to abandon Israel.

The Covenant Renewed; the Sanctuary Completed
God provided new tablets to replace the broken ones, and an abbreviated dedication ceremony was held, complete with the recitation of the laws. Much of the instruction God gave Moses on Mount Sinai prescribed the way the sanctuary was to be built and how the priests were to be costumed. All the components

were made according to these instructions and, as if to demonstrate the fidelity to these instructions, the passages in Exodus 35–39 virtually repeat those in Exodus 25–31. When everything was completed, Moses inspected the work and placed his seal of approval on it. Then the tabernacle and its protective wall were set up according to divine prescription.

It was noted earlier that the covenant was regarded as a marriage ceremony between God and his people. Now that God's residence was completed, it was ready for his glory (symbolizing God's presence) to take its place in the Holy of Holies to reside with his bride. By so doing, the second part of the patriarchal promise was completed: Israel had become a great nation, and God had truly blessed them by entering into a special relationship with them.

Wilderness Wanderings

Shortly after the tabernacle and the regulations for worship and community life were established, the Israelites approached the Promised Land of Canaan. Moses sent spies into the land before making an organized invasion. The spies reported that the land was very fruitful, but they also feared the many strong inhabitants who lived in well-fortified cities. Only Caleb and Joshua were confident that they could take the land. The people of Israel were persuaded by the reports of the other spies, and they became discouraged. They considered choosing a new leader to take them back to Egypt. God became very angry with the faithlessness of the people and condemned them to wander in the wilderness south of Canaan until that entire generation died. Joshua and Caleb were spared, however, since they were in favor of taking the land from the beginning. They would be the only ones to survive long enough to enter the Promised Land.

The book of **Numbers** records the Israelites' many experiences during their wilderness wanderings. Once Israel had finally reached the plains of Moab near the Jordan River, Moses led the people in a covenant renewal ceremony recorded in the book of **Deuteronomy.** Shortly thereafter, Moses died, and Joshua succeeded the great leader.

............THE CONQUEST OF CANAAN

After the Israelites finished their somewhat extended journey to the Promised Land, the conquest of Canaan began. Joshua led the tribes of Israel across the Jordan River and into Canaan, where many cities were taken by the Israelites over the following years. The book of **Joshua** summarizes this extremely successful time in Israel's history. During this time, general territories were established for the twelve tribes of Israel, and cities of refuge were designated. It is important to note, however, that the conquest of Canaan was never fully completed, and the Israelites lived alongside Canaanites and other peoples of the land. This failure to fully take possession of the Promised Land would come back to haunt them later.

After Joshua's death, the twelve tribes dispersed to their allotted territories where further military operations were carried out. Without centralized leadership, however, Israel slipped into a dark age characterized by military invasion, social upheaval, religious apostasy, political instability, and even civil war. The book of **Judges** documents this gloomy period. Charismatic leaders, or judges, appeared from time to time during this era to liberate certain tribes or regions from foreign oppression. The setting for the book of **Ruth** also takes place during this time period.

The period of the judges came to a close with the lives of the priest-judge Eli and his apprentice Samuel. Eli's judgeship was marred by corruption from his own sons, who were also priests, and by embarrassing military defeats at the hands of the Philistines. In the second defeat, the ark of the covenant, containing the Ten Commandments and other sacred objects, was temporarily lost to the Philistines. News of this event precipitated the death of Eli. Shiloh, the religious capital, was apparently destroyed during this time, and the returned Ark had to be placed in Kiriath-jearim until its next home was determined.

The leadership of Samuel, who succeeded Eli as priest-judge, was unique, for he combined the offices of prophet, priest, and judge. His credits include founding the first schools for the prophets and forming the link between the theocracy and the monarchy. Samuel continued to be involved in Israel's affairs until David ascended to the throne of the United Monarchy.

By the end of the period of the judges, Israel was composed of twelve autonomous tribes whose relationships had been marred by distrust, jealousy, and intertribal wars. It would be the enormous task of the first king of Israel to unite these feuding tribes into a single nation.

. . . . .THE UNITED MONARCHY (ca. 1050–970 B.C.)

The book of **1 Samuel** describes the final days of the judges and the advent of the United Monarchy. Moral corruption and tribal dissension convinced the elders of Israel that the nation needed a king in order to survive. The new king would need to be a popular, unifying figure and an able military leader in order to unite Israel and fend off the rising Philistine force in the southwest. So the elders approached Samuel to select such a person.

Saul (ca. 1051–1011 B.C.)

Saul of Benjamin was chosen to become the first king of Israel and Judah. The establishment of his kingship took place in stages. First, in a private ceremony, Samuel anointed Saul king over Israel and Judah. Second, Samuel publicly confirmed his selection of Saul by casting lots, and he formally presented the new king to the people at Mizpah. While at his home in Gibeah a few miles north of Jerusalem, Saul learned of the Ammonite

19

siege of Jabesh, an Israelite town east of the Jordan River. Empowered by the spirit of the Lord, Saul vanquished the Ammonites and earned popular support for his kingship. This third and final stage of Saul's rise to firm kingship was publicly acknowledged at Gilgal.

Meanwhile, the Philistines in the southwest continued to be a thorn in Israel's side as they had for generations. Encouraged by his own victory over the Ammonites and by his son Jonathan's victory over the Philistine garrison at Geba, Saul turned his attention to the Philistines. The Philistines held a monopoly over iron in the region, which gave them military superiority. The first encounter took place at Michmash, four miles northeast of Gibeah. Assisted by the heroism of Jonathan, Saul pushed the Philistines from the central hill country. Before the battle, however, Saul had grown impatient for Samuel to arrive and make a sacrifice, so he usurped the role of priest for himself. This religious arrogance precipitated the slow decline that characterized Saul's final years as king. It is wrong, however, to characterize Saul's reign as one of total alienation from God and of failure as a leader of his people. For approximately the first two-thirds of his reign, Saul successfully defended Israel's territory, gave God credit for victory, and worked to rid the land of religious error. Years later, however, during his victory over the Amalekites, Saul again displayed his religious insolence by disobediently sparing the vanquished King Agag and the best of the sheep and oxen.

The last few years of Saul's reign were marked by fear of his rival David, whom Samuel had anointed as Saul's successor. Although David was already king by virtue of his anointment, his introduction to the royal court came as the court musician whose duty was to soothe Saul's troubled spirit. Later, David came to public attention by his heroic victory over the Philistine giant named Goliath. When Saul recognized the popularity

David had achieved in Israel, his jealousy consumed him. He sought to kill David, forcing the anointed future king to flee for his life. In the end, Saul and three of his sons were killed on Mount Gilboa in the north of Israel while fighting the Philistines, the same nation whose defeat at Michmash brought Saul fame during the early years of his reign.

David (ca. 1011–997 B.C.)
The book of **2 Samuel** chronicles David's tumultuous ascent to the throne. Like Saul, David's path to the throne involved three stages. First, Samuel anointed him privately to the kingship, just as he had done for Saul. A period of flight from Saul ensued before the second stage was completed. After Saul had died in battle, however, David moved to Hebron in the southern hill country, where he was anointed king over Judah. Unfortunately, Saul had not succeeded in fully uniting the tribes into one nation, so for the first seven and a half years of David's rule, he was king only over Judah. Upon Saul's death, one of his sons, Ish-bosheth, had become king over Israel, that is, over the northern tribes and Benjamin.

The third stage of David's ascension was facilitated by Abner, who had been Saul's, and subsequently Ishbosheth's, military commander. Abner offered to transfer his loyalties to David for certain concessions. But before the transaction could be completed, Joab, David's commander in chief, murdered Abner in retaliation for the death of his younger brother. Events turned further in David's favor when two of Ishbosheth's officers assassinated their king and brought his head to David. Unfortunately for them, David did not appreciate that sort of help, apparently due to his deep respect for Saul's anointed position. David put both of these men to death. Nevertheless, the way was then open for David to become ruler over the entire nation. The elders of Israel gathered at Hebron to formalize an agreement making the thirty-year-old David king over both Israel and Judah. This union of the nation, more of will than of geography, was possibly the strongest national bond that had existed since the days of Moses and Joshua. Yet it became even stronger as David's leadership progressed.

One of David's best-advised domestic strategies was to capture the city of Jerusalem from the Jebusites and to move his capital there. Jerusalem was a neutral site to which he could attach the loyalties of both Israel and Judah. The city was not confined within the boundaries of an established tribal territory. It conveniently straddled the border between the tribes of Judah and Benjamin.

The national confidence engendered by this valiant leader proved justified as David tackled the relentless Philistine menace. Perceiving David to be a threat to their political dominance, the Philistines made a preemptive strike against Israel, south of Jerusalem in the valley of Rephaim. David's stunning victory in this battle caused the Philistines to flee for their lives. A second decisive victory in this same location finally ended Philistine domination.

Shortly after the second victory over the Philistines, David moved the ark of the covenant to Jerusalem. God then established a covenant with David. He promised David that his house, or lineage, would never be removed from the earth, unlike Saul's family. Thus, God adopted David as a son and promised to watch over him and discipline him as a father would discipline his child.

King David's charismatic personality and exemplary military prowess enabled him to consolidate the nation of Israel both religiously and politically. He commanded the nearly unswerving loyalty of his subjects and militarists, including his three nephews, Joab, Abishai, and Asahel, whose military expertise and personal friendship were David's mainstays throughout his reign.

The personal loyalty and effective army that David established made a program of expansionism possible. David's administrative strategy was to establish a military garrison in each conquered territory in order to keep a tight reign on his empire. He broadened Israel's economic base by collecting heavy tribute from conquered countries. Much of this new income was necessarily reinvested in the maintenance of military garrisons, but some of it was used to acquire building materials from King Hiram of Tyre. David was building a new palace in Jerusalem and was planning to build a temple there as well. To the east and southeast he conducted successful military campaigns against Moab and Edom, gaining access to the Gulf of Aqaba. This southern waterway gave Israel a new trade route, thus widening the commercial potential that Solomon would later develop. In the northern extremities, King David launched a military campaign against King Rehob of Zobah, north of Damascus. When the campaign was over, David had gained control of both Zobah and Damascus. Then the king of Hamath, a province north of Zobah, began paying voluntary tribute to David.

At some point in the expansion program, Joab, David's general, conducted a successful campaign against Ammon, on the eastern side of the Jordan, to consolidate Israelite control of the Transjordan. During this military operation, David stayed at home in Jerusalem, where he became adulterously involved with Bathsheba. Tragically, the child that came from this relationship died soon after birth. Not long after this affair, David's son Absalom rebelled against his father and attempted to overthrow him. Again, the sad result of this heartbreaking incident was the death of David's beloved son. This was possibly the lowest period of David's life.

Despite his moral failures, David was called a "man after [God's] own heart" (1 Samuel 13:14). Even regarding his own faults, David expressed an acute sense of right and wrong and passionately desired to please God. This passion for God can be found in the book of **Psalms,** half of which are traditionally credited to David. The psalms are Hebrew worship songs that were sung at various occasions and ceremonies, some public, others private. The moods of the psalms range anywhere from sorrow and lament to praise and celebration.

After a very long and prosperous reign over Israel, David's career came to a close as he became very old and feeble. Unable to keep warm and losing energy to continue living, David made plans to pass on the crown.

Solomon (ca. 971–931 B.C.)

SECURING THE THRONE   The transition from the end of David's reign to the prosperous reign of Solomon is recounted in the first half of the book of **1 Kings.** As David lay gravely ill, his eldest surviving son, Adonijah, held a coronation dinner to acclaim himself king with the support of Joab, David's military commander, and the high priest Abiathar. In the meantime, hastened by the news of this self-coronation, Bathsheba and the prophet Nathan petitioned David to proclaim Solomon, the son of Bathsheba and David, king. So, before Adonijah's coronation feast was concluded, Solomon was crowned king, and Adonijah fled to the sanctuary, where he took refuge at the altar. Solomon spared his life, but soon after David's death, Adonijah made another attempt to usurp the throne. This time Solomon took vengeance and killed him.

Solomon took further steps to secure his rule. He executed Joab for his excessive bloodshed and support of Adonijah; he banished Abiathar to his home in Anathoth; and he restricted Shimei, David's long-standing enemy, to Jerusalem, so he would not spread his discontent. Shimei agreed to Solomon's order but eventually ventured out of Jerusalem to retrieve some runaway

slaves. Solomon, true to his word, had his new military commander, Benaiah, kill Shimei. Though it may seem cruel to many
readers today that so much killing should attend a new king's
ascent to the throne, it was a reality of the ancient world. An
orderly transfer of power was the exception, not the rule. Solomon, though a man of peace, was not a man of indecision. He
knew that his kingdom was insecure so long as old enemies and
rivals harbored grudges and aspirations for the throne.

Solomon was not a warrior like his father, but he strengthened
his defenses by fortifying key cities to guard the entrances to
Israel's heartland. These cities included Gezer, Beth-horon,
Hazor in the north, Megiddo in the Plain of Esdraelon, and
Baalath on the western border with Philistia. He also expanded
Israel's use of the chariot, a military asset used only minimally
by his father.

SOLOMON'S ADMINISTRATIVE GENIUS   The complexities of
ruling a vast kingdom proved to be no obstruction to Solomon's
ambitions. He seemed to enjoy the challenge. In order to hold
the empire together, Solomon strengthened his defenses as a
deterrent to war, expanded the diplomatic policy begun by his
father, and sealed foreign alliances by marriage between the ally-
ing royal houses. A king whose daughter was married to Solomon would think twice before launching a revolt. Two of
Solomon's most important marriage alliances were with Egypt
and Tyre.

A second challenge for Solomon was keeping his own people
content. There is good reason to believe that Solomon began his
reign with a deep desire to be understanding and wise. He
acquired national and international acclaim for his wisdom. As
Solomon's prosperity grew, however, he became increasingly
insensitive to the needs of his own people and ended his days
with a gluttonous appetite for his own pleasure.

Providing for his immense court, which catered to seven hundred wives and three hundred concubines, proved to be yet another colossal task for Solomon. Maintaining costly military networks and extensive building projects also placed a heavy burden on the ambitious king. To oversee the intricate web of operations in his kingdom, Solomon expanded his administrative cabinet and divided the country into twelve administrative districts. Each district provided for the court's needs for one month each year. In order to maintain an adequate labor force for his building projects, Solomon conscripted Canaanites as well as Israelites as a source of free labor. The system functioned well, but the basic concept was flawed, and eventually such practices levied so great a toll on the northern tribes that they seceded from the kingdom upon Solomon's death.

A CULTURAL RENAISSANCE   David had left an expanded, stable kingdom for Solomon. At the time of David's death, the neighboring states were relatively weak, giving Solomon a political and economic advantage over them. Unlike David, Solomon had been reared in the court and most likely had leisure time for educational pursuits. Solomon's highly educated background, the internal stability of his kingdom, the influx of foreigners, and the extensive international commerce during his reign brought a new level of cultural opportunity and cultivation to Israel. One aspect of that cultural renaissance can be seen in Solomon's architectural accomplishments in Jerusalem. These included a magnificent temple built with imported materials, an armory called the "Palace of the Forest of Lebanon," his own royal palace, the "Hall of Pillars" (perhaps a connecting promenade), and a "Hall of Judgment," where administrative and judicial functions took place. For twenty years the architectural form and aesthetic beauty of these buildings took shape before the eyes of those in Jerusalem. Solomon also encouraged literary pursuits and even

composed and collected songs. Three books have been traditionally associated with Solomon's authorship: **Proverbs,
Ecclesiastes,** and the **Song of Songs.**

. . . . .THE EARLY DIVIDED KINGDOM (931–841 B.C.)

The second half of 1 Kings and the first half of **2 Kings**
document the years of the Divided Kingdoms of Israel and
Judah. Prior to the Divided Kingdom, there are very few definite
dates to form a skeleton upon which to hang various events
recorded in the Bible. From the Divided Kingdom onward, however, the chronological data is extremely complete, and several
synchronisms can be made with extrabiblical history. At first
study, this wealth of data seems spattered with error. Discrepancies in such matters as the length of certain reigns have given
rise to two extreme conclusions: that there must be some mysti-
cal meaning in the numbers, or that the text must certainly be
flawed. Although some scholars still hold to these conclusions,
major research has since uncovered some of the principles upon
which ancient chronology was based and has helped scholars
more accurately interpret the biblical data. In brief, ancient Near
Eastern chronology computed the reign of kings slightly differ-
ently than modern dating methods, and this often leads to discrepancies between ancient and modern calculations. Not every
chronological citation can be clarified, but since the vast majority of discrepancies have been resolved, wholesale emendations
of the text are no longer warranted.

Rehoboam and Jeroboam

Rehoboam was crown prince when his father, Solomon, died.
For some unspecified reason, Rehoboam chose Shechem, rather
than Jerusalem, for his coronation ceremony. At Shechem Rehoboam listened to the advice of his young friends rather than that
of the elders and refused the people's request to lighten the tax

burden placed on them by his father. The resulting uproar and revolt reflects back on Solomon's reign and shows how fragile the kingdom had become by the time of his death. The northern tribes deserted, and Rehoboam became king only of Judah, the southern tribe.

Jeroboam was chosen king over the new northern nation of Israel. Northern Israel had several advantages over the kingdom of Judah. Israel claimed over three quarters of the combined land area, and their territory had the best pasturage and farmland in all of Palestine. The north had continued access to the Mediterranean and to the trade routes between Aram (Syria) and Egypt. Judah, on the other hand, was landlocked and located off the main trade routes. Lastly, Israel's ten tribes contained far more inhabitants than Judah. Judah retained Jerusalem, the old capital city, with its accumulated wealth and the temple. Nevertheless, Israel began as the stronger of the two nations.

Rehoboam initially attempted to incite a civil war between the two rival kingdoms but backed off when a prophet declared that the split had been ordained by God. Repeatedly throughout the rest of Old Testament history, prophets would influence or try to influence contemporary events.

Rehoboam remained peacefully in his capital city of Jerusalem for a time, and Jeroboam fortified Shechem as his capital. The location of the temple at Jerusalem, however, made Jeroboam uneasy. He feared that his subjects might defect if they had to travel to Jerusalem for worship. To eliminate this concern, Jeroboam instituted several substitutes designed to keep the people in their home territory. Golden calves were set up at Bethel and Dan, with Jeroboam acting as high priest for Israel, and the border with Judah was closed. Canaanite worship centers, or "high places," were also established, and priesthoods were put on the trading block rather than being confined to the Levitical tribe. In protest to these changes, many Levites and other "faithful" Israelites began emigrating south into Judah. Other Levites were forcibly thrown out of Israel.

The books of 1 and 2 Kings make a point to rate each king of Israel and Judah as either "good" or "bad," based primarily upon religious criteria, even though some "bad" kings apparently made many positive economic and political contributions to the kingdom. Every single king of northern Israel received a "bad" rating, while Judah had some "good" kings as well as "bad" ones.

At first, Rehoboam's kingdom remained fairly faithful to the religious practices established under David. As time wore on, however, high places and pillars to Canaanite deities began appearing in Judah. Near the end of Rehoboam's reign, Shishak, king of Egypt, marched on Judah. Only a few years earlier Egypt had found it necessary to maintain good relations with its northern neighbor. Now Shishak, founder of the Twenty-second Dynasty in Egypt, despoiled Jerusalem and the Judean countryside. Extrabiblical texts and archaeology add that Egyptian forces continued into northern Israel as well.

The Remainder of the Early Divided Kingdom
The next decades of the Early Divided Kingdom can become confusing for readers who are unfamiliar with this time period, but the following summary should help to clarify how Israel and Judah dealt with each other, how the outside world affected their histories, and which prophets fit into this time period. Such emphases will provide the interested reader with a basis for more detailed study in the future.

Israel and Judah continued to engage in border skirmishes, and Judah appears to have held the upper hand in most instances, despite the seemingly stronger position of Israel. A clear landmark victory was won for Judah when the important cult center of Bethel was wrested from Israel during the reign of Abijah.

Asa was Judah's first "good" king, and, consequently, God

granted him peace and protection. For example, in Asa's fourteenth year Egypt sent another army led by Zerah to raid Palestine, and God responded to Asa's prayer for help by enabling Judah to rout the Egyptians. Zerah is not called the king or Pharaoh by the biblical writers, and thus he is likely a mercenary general who acted for King Osorkon I. This was the second time Egypt entered the history of the Early Divided Kingdom, and it would continue to menace Judah for the next several centuries. But throughout the remainder of the Old Testament, Egypt was not a major threat until the final decades of Judah's history.

A year after Egypt's invasion was turned back, Baasha, king of Israel, began to build a fort at Ramah, only five miles north of Jerusalem. Asa believed Judah was being threatened again, so he bribed Benhadad, king of Aram, to attack Israel and force Baasha to pull his troops north.

Benhadad's army invaded northern Israel and, as Asa hoped, diverted Baasha from Judah. Although Asa's action maintained the political well-being of Judah, it came at great personal price. When a prophet pointed out to Asa that he should have depended on God for protection, the king reacted in anger. For the remainder of his long reign, Asa was given a "bad" rating.

Thanks to Asa, Judah continued to be stronger than Israel. But Asa's action impacted Israel beyond the immediate incident at Ramah, setting in motion a pattern of Aramean interest and intervention in Palestine. Aram became the dominant threat to Israel during the Early Divided Kingdom.

Israel and Judah contrast sharply regarding the stability of their ruling houses. In Judah, the Davidic line continued to reign unbroken until the fall of Jerusalem in 586 B.C. In Israel, however, new dynasties murdered their way to the throne on several occasions. The first example of this occurred when Elah succeeded his father, Baasha. Shortly after Elah came to power, he was murdered by Zimri, one of his chariot commanders. In typical fashion for such coups of the Near East, Zimri killed all the royal relatives and friends. By this bloodbath Zimri hoped to secure the throne for himself, but it turned out that Zimri lacked the support of Omri, commander of the army. Omri marched on the capital, and Zimri was forced to commit suicide after a reign of only seven days. The details are not clear, but it seems that the next five years were fraught with civil war between Omri and the followers of a man named Tibni. Omri eventually secured his reign over all Israel.

A few noteworthy events occurred in Omri's reign. For example, Omri moved Israel's capital to Samaria. This is already the third capital for the northern nation; for a time it had been at Tirzah. Samaria remained the capital city until the fall of the Northern Kingdom in 722 B.C. During Omri's reign there is no mention of war between Israel and Judah. This seems to be the first glimpse of a friendship that would later develop between the two nations.

As noted above, Egypt invaded Judah twice within the opening decades of the Divided Kingdom, and Aram had its interest in Israel awakened by King Asa. In 876 B.C., during the reign of Omri, Assyria faintly entered the Near Eastern scene when King Assurnasirpal reached the Mediterranean with his army. For centuries afterward Israel was known in Assyrian texts as the "land of Omri." Assyrian intelligence probably did little more than learn that a nation ruled by a king named Omri was to the south of their march. First contact had been made, however, and that contact would increase late in the Early Divided Kingdom.

Omri was followed by his son, Ahab. The Bible judges Ahab as one of the worst Israelite kings. Both Omri and Ahab sponsored the worship of the Canaanite deities Baal and Asherah. Politically, however, Ahab was one of Israel's stronger rulers. He fended off an Aramean attack on his capital and even captured the king of Aram. Nevertheless, Judah continued to be the stronger of the two nations, as evidenced by the Judean forts built in territory initially belonging to Israel.

Omri had arranged the marriage of his son, Ahab, to the Phoenician princess, Jezebel. Having been raised in a country where royalty was not to be denied, Jezebel could not understand why Ahab merely sulked when he could not obtain the vineyard of Naboth. Jezebel simply seized the vineyard for Ahab by arranging the murder of its owner.

Jezebel's zeal for her Phoenician god caused a clash between the royal family and the prophet Elijah. Because of the wickedness of Israel and the royal family, Elijah predicted a drought that would last three and a half years. During this time, Ahab desperately tried to convince Elijah to recant the curse on his kingdom. Elijah finally called for a test of strength between himself, the prophet of God, and the hundreds of prophets of Baal and Asherah. In the confrontation atop Mount Carmel, God demonstrated his superiority before the assembled people, and the prophets of Baal and Asherah were then killed. When Elijah heard that Jezebel wanted him dead, however, he panicked and fled all the way to Mount Sinai. God revealed himself to Elijah there and told him to return to Israel and continue his ministry.

Ahab played an important role in one of the famous battles of antiquity. The Battle of Karkar (853 B.C.) is not recorded in the Bible. That year the Assyrian king, Shalmaneser III, was trying to carve out an empire, and several local kings gathered in Karkar of Aram to try to stop Assyria's westward advance. The famous Black Obelisk of Shalmaneser III relates that fifty thousand troops were drawn up against the Assyrians and that Ahab fielded the second largest army in that coalition. Only the Aramean army was larger than Ahab's. Much blood and rhetoric flowed before the battle was over, and the Assyian annals claim great victory. A less biased analysis notes, however, that the Assyrian advance stalled at Karkar. At best it would seem the Assyrians won at considerable cost. The Battle of Karkar shows a side of Ahab's reign the biblical writers were not interested in recording and represents the first physical contact between Israel and Assyria. Israel never again fared as well in its contacts with Assyria.

The pivotal battle of Ramoth-gilead was fought during the same year as the Battle of Karkar. Ahab decided to use his already assembled army to take Ramoth-gilead, an important trade city in Aram. Ahab asked Jehoshaphat, king of Judah, if he would join forces in battle. Jehoshaphat reluctantly agreed, becoming a decoy to lure the enemy away from Ahab. The campaign was a failure, and Ahab died on the battlefield. By the time of the battle, Israel had become stronger than Judah.

Jehoshaphat continued to have contacts with Israel. In one episode, King Ahaziah of the Northern Kingdom asked for help to build a fleet that would sail south for gold. Jehoshaphat agreed, only to have God destroy the ships. Another time, King Joram wanted to retake control of Moab. Jehoshaphat again agreed to lend assistance, but the battle foundered.

During Joram's reign, Elisha succeeded the prophet Elijah. One of Elisha's miracles involved curing an Aramean military officer of leprosy. While the point of the miracle was primarily religious, there was also a political sidelight. Tensions were high between Israel and Aram, but Israel no longer had a king who was able to field a strong army. Aramean army units were able to move virtually unchallenged within Israel.

The bloody transfers of power that characterized Israel seeped over into Judah during the final years of the Early Divided Kingdom. Jehoram served as coregent for a time with his father, Jehoshaphat, but when Jehoshaphat died, Jehoram tried to solidify his hold on the throne by killing all six of his brothers. His reign continued to be filled with political unrest. There were revolts in Judah's dependencies, and a few raids were made on Jerusalem.

In one raid, Jehoram lost all but one of his sons. Through this one son, Ahaziah, the Davidic line was preserved. Ahaziah only reigned for a short time, however, and he followed the counsel of his idolatrous mother, Athaliah. Athaliah was the daughter of Ahab and Jezebel and had been given in marriage to Jehoram to seal a political alliance between Israel and Judah. The biblical writers rated Ahaziah as "bad."

The Early Divided Kingdom came to a close around 841 B.C. In that year Ahaziah, king of Judah, and his uncle Joram, king of Israel, advanced on Ramoth-gilead to take it from Aramean control. During the course of the battle, Joram received a wound and retired to his summer palace in Jezreel to recuperate. Ahaziah left the battle to visit Joram.

While the two kings were at Jezreel, Elisha sent a prophet to Jehu, an army captain of the troops besieging Ramoth-gilead. The prophet secretly anointed Jehu as the new king of Israel and commanded him to destroy the house of Ahab for its sins. When pressed, Jehu disclosed to his men what the prophet had done and said. Jehu and a company of men then sped west some thirty miles to Jezreel. Joram was unsuspecting of the coup attempt until it was too late, and he was struck dead in his chariot. Ahaziah tried to escape, but he, too, was mortally wounded.

Jehu entered Jezreel, where Jezebel was residing. She began to taunt him but was cast down from the palace to her death. Jehu ordered the execution of Ahab's seventy sons and killed a large number of Ahab's leaders, friends, and priests. Jehu also destroyed all the Baal worshipers in the land. The speed of the coup was such that relatives of Ahaziah who were coming north to meet with the king were also caught in the bloodbath. The simultaneous deaths of the kings of both Israel and Judah marks the close of the Early Divided Kingdom.

During the ninety years of the Early Divided Kingdom, the political relations between Israel and Judah went from warring to warming to close friendship. For most of the period, Judah was able to maintain military superiority. It was only after the two royal houses had intermarried that Judah became the weaker nation. During the Early Divided Kingdom Egypt played only a minor role in the history of Palestine. Assyria had made contact but had not yet set foot in the country. Aram, however, repeatedly was a major threat to Israel.

. . . . .THE LATE DIVIDED KINGDOM (841–722 B.C.)

Years of Weakness
Israel's four dynasties prior to Jehu had been relatively short, while Jehu's dynasty proved to be the longest in Israel's history. His radical purge of the house of Omri, though accomplishing its purpose, created a vacuum of capable leaders in Israel and thereby greatly weakened the country. Jehu's religious zeal that tore down the powerful Baal cult fell short of returning his kingdom to the true worship of God, since he did not abandon the debilitating religious practices instituted by Jeroboam. This particular failure earned Jehu the same "bad" rating as all the other kings of Israel.

Repercussions of Jehu's policies soon became evident. The diplomatic alliances upon which Omri and Ahab had built their foreign policy began to collapse, severing critical ties with Phoenicia and with Judah. Israel and Judah would never again have friendly relations as separate nations.

Jehu's reign was further weakened by strong pressures from the north. During the first year of Jehu's reign, Shalmaneser III campaigned west again. This is the same Assyrian king whose advance was stalled at Karkar twelve years earlier by Ahab and his coalition of forces. This time no coalition formed to meet the Assyrians, and Israel was forced to pay tribute to Assyria for several years. After another western campaign three years later, the

Assyrians did not return to Israel for over thirty years. Their absence left the door wide open for the Arameans to wrest all of the Transjordan from Israel.

In Judah, when Athaliah saw her opportunity to seize the throne of her dead son, she killed her grandsons who were in line to succeed him. She took the throne herself and became the first and only non-Davidic ruler to reign in Judah. Despite her seemingly thorough purge, the priest Jehoiada and his wife rescued one royal infant, Joash, and hid him from the queen's wrath. After Athaliah had reigned six years, Jehoiada arranged a coup. He publicly presented Joash, who was only seven years old at the time, elevated him to the kingship, and ordered the execution of Athaliah.

The reign of Joash overlapped much of Jehu's kingship in Israel. Under the strong influence of the priest, Jehoiada, Joash conducted a religious reform in Judah, eliminating the Baal cult that Athaliah had popularized. Joash reinstituted pure worship of God and reinstalled the Levitical priests and temple personnel. He also initiated needful repairs of the temple, which had been plundered for its treasures by Athaliah's sons. Joash's religious zeal was fanned by Jehoiada's fervor, but when the priest died toward the end of Joash's long reign, idolatry became a factor in Judah once again.

About midway through Joash's reign in Judah, Jehoahaz succeeded his father, Jehu, as king of Israel. Elisha had predicted that Hazael, king of Aram, would ravage Israel, and this prophecy was fulfilled during Jehoahaz's reign. Repeated Aramean incursions weakened Israel to the point that Hazael could dictate the size of Israel's army. Aram's forays even reached into Judah, and on one campaign Hazael captured Gath and would have proceeded to Jerusalem had not King Joash bought him off with gold obtained from the temple and from the royal treasury. Aramean pressures caused Jehoahaz to temporarily seek help from

God, who provided Israel with a "deliverer." This "deliverer" can perhaps be identified as the Assyrian king Adad-nirari III. In 803 B.C. he besieged Aram's capital city, Damascus, and thereby forced Aram to pull its troops out of Israel in order to defend its own territories. This event marked the end of Aram's domination of Israel.

The end of Aramean dominance made a positive difference in Israel during the reign of Jehoahaz's son, Jehoash. Encouraged by the aged prophet Elisha, Jehoash turned his attention to the recovery of all the Israelite cities that had been lost to Aram.

The new political situation impacted the fortunes of Judah as well. In Judah, King Amaziah, son of Joash, launched a campaign against the Edomites and was victorious, but then he foolishly brought their gods back to Jerusalem and worshiped them. Next, he unwisely challenged Israel in battle. Jehoash of Israel tried to dissuade his Judean counterpart, but Amaziah attacked anyway and was captured. He was kept at Samaria for several years before being allowed to return home. Uzziah began to reign in place of his imprisoned father.

Jehoash was followed by his capable son, Jeroboam II, during whose reign Israel reached a new plateau in history. Jeroboam, an able military strategist, restored the borders of Israel to the northern and eastern limits of the previous United Kingdom. Israel's expansion was possible, in part, because of the weakness of Aram to the north and Assyria to the northeast.

Judah began to experience prosperity under the capable leadership of Uzziah. Judah continued to control Edom in the south and established a port at Elath on the Gulf of Aqaba, thus widening Judah's commercial potential. Uzziah strengthened Judah's defenses, and new settlements were established in much of the Negev.

Recovery and Advancement; the Prophets Jonah, Amos, and Hosea
The transition between the periods of the Early Divided Kingdom and the Late Divided Kingdom also marked the transition
from preclassical prophecy to classical prophecy. Preclassical
refers to prophecy before the eighth century B.C. and included
such influential figures as Nathan, Elijah, and Elisha. Some common characteristics of these early prophets are that none of them
has a book bearing his name and oracles; that the king, rather
than the people, was the target of their censures; and that they
proclaimed messages of judgment more often than calls to repentance. Classical prophets, on the other hand, were active after the
eighth century B.C., and their oracles can be found in books
named after them. They typically addressed the people and
called them to repent of their wicked actions. Jonah, Amos, and
Hosea are the first of these classical prophets.

The prophecies of **Jonah** place themselves near the period of
Jeroboam II's reign, anywhere from 810 to 754 B.C. during a time
of Assyrian weakness. We know very little about this prophet's personal life except that his father was named Amittai and his hometown was Gath-hepher, near Nazareth of Galilee. Many consider
the book of Jonah to be purely allegorical and do not think that
the events actually took place as they are recorded. Nevertheless,
the book of 2 Kings does refer to him as an actual person.

After obstinately completing a circuitous route to Nineveh, the
capital of Assyria, Jonah preached a message of condemnation to
the people, shouting, "Forty days from now Nineveh will be
destroyed!" Jonah prophesied against their wicked cruelty and
their belief in many false gods. Jonah himself did not actually
want to see the Assyrians escape judgment, and he became angry
when the people did repent and God chose to recant his curse on
the city.

The prophets **Amos** and **Hosea** provide added insight into the
prosperous times of Uzziah and Jeroboam II. Both prophets con-

demned Jeroboam for his godless policies, which ignored God's demands and winked at the social sins that plagued his nation. They reveal that, for both nations, moral decline and religious indifference accompanied the years of peace and prosperity.

Amos came from a village in Judah, where he was a shepherd and tender of sycamore trees. Despite his humble beginnings, around 765 B.C. Amos stepped into Israel's notorious sanctuary at Bethel to indict the neighbors of Israel, the greedy oppressors of the poor, and Jeroboam II of the Northern Kingdom, whose nation was filled with moral decay in spite of its political achievement. The prophet warned of the impending "day of the Lord" and of the destruction awaiting the nation of Israel if it did not repent. Amos's message was not well received at Bethel, and the priest Amaziah accused him of plotting against Jeroboam.

The prophets' personal involvement in their message is best exemplified by Hosea. Hosea's marriage to a prostitute (possibly of a religious cult) and the subsequent birth of his children symbolized Israel's unfaithfulness to God. The unfaithfulness of Hosea's wife caused him to send her away. Hosea then paid the price of a slave to redeem his former wife from degradation, and their relationship was renewed. These actions symbolized God's love for Israel. Although God had to divorce himself from Israel because of her sins, his love for Israel did not fail and the separation was not permanent. Hosea most likely lived during the reigns of Uzziah, Jotham, Ahaz, and Hezekiah and prophesied near the popular sanctuaries of Israel, such as Bethel, Dan, Gilgal, and Samaria.

The Fall of Israel and the Decline of Judah

The Jehu dynasty of Israel, begun in 841 B.C., came to an end in 753 B.C. when Jeroboam's son, Zechariah, died. After only six months on the throne he was assassinated by a usurper named Shallum. Shallum had ruled only one month when he, in turn, was assassinated by another usurper named Menahem. Political instability characterized the years following Jeroboam's death, and, as a consequence, Israel was unable to withstand the imperial ambitions of the new Assyrian king, Tiglath-pileser III, who is called by his Babylonian throne name, Pul, in the book of 2 Kings. Menahem was forced to pay a humiliating tribute to this emperor around 743 B.C., and so he exacted fifty shekels of silver from every wealthy man in Israel. This capital campaign produced the exorbitant sum of one thousand silver talents (3 million shekels), which implies there were sixty thousand wealthy men in Israel. This brought an end to the period of prosperity in the Northern Kingdom.

Menahem's son and successor, Pekahiah, had ruled for two years when he was assassinated by one of his officials named Pekah. During Pekah's kingship, Tiglath-pileser again campaigned in the west. Ahaz was then coregent of Judah with his father, Jotham, son of Uzziah. When he declined the invitation of Aram and Israel to join them in an alliance against Assyria, the two northern kings besieged Jerusalem. Against the advice of the prophet Isaiah, Ahaz petitioned Tiglath-pileser for help against the invaders. The Assyrian king complied and extended his conquests to the south. He annexed Aram and the northern half of Israel and forced Judah to acknowledge Assyria's superior power. Tiglath-pileser began the Assyrian policy of deporting conquered populations to distant lands within the empire, and thousands of people from the northern tribes were marched into exile. By relocating native inhabitants, Assyria hoped to dilute nationalism within the occupied lands and to sever the people from their local gods, whose power was believed to be confined within their national boundaries.

Meanwhile in Judah, Ahaz began patronizing the Baal cult and even offered human sacrifices in the valley of the son of Hinnom near Jerusalem. Ahaz lost much of the political power his predecessors had gained. As a result of this decline, the Edomites successfully revolted and took Judeans captive, the Philistines freely conducted border raids in the low hill country, and Aram captured the important seaport of Elath. Near the beginning of Ahaz's reign in Judah (732 B.C.), Pekah of Israel was assassinated by Hoshea. Tiglath-pileser was most likely behind the coup since he took credit for putting Hoshea on the throne.

Upon Tiglath-pileser's death in 727 B.C., many vassal states, including Israel, declared their freedom from Assyrian control. Hoshea withheld tribute from Assyria as he sought help from Egypt. Tiglath-pileser's son, Shalmaneser V, began his rule, however, with the same determination as his father and pulled the vassal states back into line. Shalmaneser launched his campaign against Israel in 724 B.C., Egypt withheld military support, and Hoshea was captured. Shalmaneser laid siege to Israel's capital city of Samaria and finally took it in 722 B.C., after two years of bitter resistance. With the fall of Samaria, the kingdom of Israel came to an end. According to Assyria's own records, Sargon II deported 27,290 citizens of Samaria to other parts of the Assyrian Empire.

Throughout the Late Divided Kingdom, Egypt played only a minor role in the histories of Israel and Judah. Aram continued to exert strong pressure on both kingdoms but then weakened and even became Israel's ally against Assyria. Although there were periods of weakness, Assyria eventually became the dominant power during the Late Divided Kingdom. Assyria exacted tribute from Israel, deported the population, annexed part of the land, and destroyed the nation.

During the Late Divided Kingdom, prophets continued to rail against the wickedness of the Northern Kingdom. Although the political history of Israel offers external reasons for the country's demise, the religious history poses clear internal reasons for Israel's downfall. Apostasy against the God of Abraham, Isaac, and

Jacob began with Jeroboam I (represented in part by the golden calves at Dan and Bethel) and continued unabated through the decades. The time had finally come for judgment to be executed. For Israel, however, judgment was mercifully coupled with the promise of restoration.

JUDAH ALONE (722–586 B.C.)

When Ahaz, threatened by the kings of Aram and Israel, appealed to the Assyrian king for help in 735 B.C., he unavoidably indebted himself to Assyria, and the Assyrians would not let him forget it. As long as the Assyrian Empire was strong, Judah lived under its intimidating shadow. When Ahaz died in 715 B.C., he passed this dubious legacy on to his son, Hezekiah.

Hezekiah and His Religious Reforms
The fall of Samaria, which marked the demise of the Northern Kingdom, sounded a warning signal to Judah to reshape its moral and spiritual condition. While Ahaz was hardly the man to correctly interpret this signal, his son, Hezekiah (715–686 B.C.), understood it clearly. In response to God's judgment on the Northern Kingdom, Hezekiah instigated a religious reform that reopened the temple, removed the pagan cult objects there, and reinstituted Mosaic sacrifices. Moreover, he extended this renewal not only to Judeans but also to Israelites, who now had no central government or sanctuary. Hezekiah called them together at Jerusalem to celebrate the Passover. His reformation eliminated the pagan cult centers for which the land had become known and reorganized and revitalized the priests and Levites. So thorough and sincere was Hezekiah's reform that the writer of 2 Kings calls him an imitator of his ancestor David, a distinction accorded to only three other Judean kings: Asa, Jehoshaphat, and Josiah.

As he worked to reverse his father's pro-Assyrian policy, Hezekiah was careful not to act imprudently toward the Assyrians as long as Sargon II was emperor (722–705 B.C.). In 711 B.C. the Philistine city of Ashdod, with Egyptian encouragement, invited Judah, Edom, and Moab to join a revolt against Sargon. Hezekiah declined, and consequently Judah was spared the revenge that Sargon unleashed upon Ashdod.

Upon Sargon's death, however, Hezekiah and certain Assyrian satellite states tested the power and determination of the new emperor Sennacherib. Led by the king of Tyre and urged on by the Egyptian king, Shabaka, this revolt posed a formidable challenge to the new emperor. To prepare for Sennacherib's anticipated invasion, Hezekiah strengthened Jerusalem's fortifications and dug a tunnel through bedrock to channel water from the Spring of Gihon to a place inside the city walls. The workmen engineered the project from both ends of the tunnel, working toward each other until they met somewhere in the middle. It was an impressive symbol of Hezekiah's determination to resist Assyria.

As anticipated, Sennacherib marched westward in 701 B.C., first settling accounts with Tyre, then moving on to Ashkelon, and then laying siege to Lachish on his way to Jerusalem. Hezekiah tried to appease Sennacherib by paying him tribute while the Assyrians were still at Lachish. Hezekiah had to rob the temple of its silver treasures in order to pay it. Before moving on to Jerusalem, Sennacherib fought with the Egyptian general Tirhakah while he sent a threatening letter to Hezekiah. As Hezekiah laid the letter before the Lord in the temple and invoked God's deliverance, the prophet Isaiah reassured Hezekiah that Sennacherib would withdraw. The Assyrian king recorded that he captured forty-six cities of Judah and shut Hezekiah up in Jerusalem "like a bird in a cage." Perhaps alluding to a plague that spread among the soldiers, 2 Kings records that the "angel of the Lord" went forth at night and killed 185,000 Assyrian soldiers.

Other satellites of Assyria tested the mettle of Sennacherib as well. During the reign of Hezekiah, the Chaldeans, who lived near the mouth of the Euphrates, had twice placed Merodach-baladan on the throne of the city of Babylon. He had been exiled to Elam by Sargon II in 710 B.C. and had reappeared in Babylon upon Sennacherib's elevation to the throne.

In approximately 703 B.C. Hezekiah became deathly ill, and Isaiah instructed him to put his affairs in order because he would not survive. But when the king pleaded for God's mercy, his life was extended for fifteen years. Soon after his recovery, Merodach-baladan sent messengers with the ostensible purpose of congratulating him, but more likely, he wanted to test Hezekiah's feelings concerning an anti-Assyrian pact.

Manasseh and Religious Apostasy

The religious and political policies of Hezekiah were reversed by his son Manasseh during his long reign (687–643 B.C.), and Judah's downfall was sealed. Manasseh rebuilt the foreign sanctuaries torn down by Hezekiah, erected altars to the fertility god Baal, and erected a statue of the fertility goddess Asherah. Though the prophet Isaiah was probably active until 681 B.C., there is no evidence that the king ever consulted Isaiah as Hezekiah had done.

Judah seemed to fare no better politically than it had religiously under Manasseh's reign. Although more accommodating than his father to Assyria's passion for control of the west, Manasseh was still required to pay Esar-haddon of Assyria a tribute in the year 676 B.C. He was probably also involved in a multinational revolt against Ashurbanipal during the years 652–648 B.C. Manasseh was forced to submit and was most likely taken captive to Babylonia by the Assyrian army. Remaining there for a time, Manasseh had a change of heart and asked for God's mercy. When he was restored to his throne, his religious policies were much more like his father's. His long idolatrous reign, however, had made such an impression on the nation that these final years of religious zeal could not reverse the religious state of affairs.

Josiah and His Religious Reforms

When Manasseh died, his son Amon succeeded him and reversed his father's brief reform effort. Discord in the royal house, however, resulted in Amon's assassination after a two-year reign (643–641 B.C.).

Josiah was only eight years old when he succeeded his father Amon. At the age of sixteen, Josiah turned his attention to spiritual matters, and at age twenty he initiated a religious reform to remove the Baal cult from Judah and to restore true worship to the God of his ancestor David. Some scholars believe that the prophetic ministry of Zephaniah was a spiritual encouragement to this king. Neither the book of Zephaniah nor the historical books make this connection, except to date the prophet in Josiah's reign.

Josiah's reform, begun in 628 B.C, first targeted Judah and then extended into Israel. Josiah executed the priests of Baal and purged Bethel of the cult located there. A compromise was made for the rural priests of the Baal cult in Judah by transferring the priests to Jerusalem, where they served at the temple in subsidiary roles. In 622 B.C. the fires of reform were further fueled by the discovery of the Book of the Law during repairs to the temple. When the prophetess Huldah was consulted about its authenticity, she confirmed it and prophesied the destruction of Judah, promising that Josiah would be spared the painful experience of seeing the actual downfall of the nation.

Josiah's reform came in a time of political transition in the

Near East. By 622 B.C. the Assyrian Empire was declining, and ominous signs pointed to a Chaldean-dominated world. In 626 B.C. the Assyrian-appointed governor of Babylon died, and a Chaldean usurper, Nabopolassar, seized the Babylonian throne. With the assistance of the Medes, the Chaldeans removed the vestiges of the Assyrian Empire and captured Asshur in 614 B.C. and Nineveh in 612 B.C.

Josiah was killed at Megiddo in 609 B.C. during a battle with the Egyptians. His death virtually terminated all reforms. For a brief time Pharaoh Neco II of Egypt held the balance of power in the ancient Near East, but by this time Judah's fate was already sealed. In 605 B.C. the Babylonian army (including the Chaldeans) won a decisive victory over the Egyptian army in a battle at Carchemish on the Euphrates River. Nebuchadnezzar, ruling in the absence of his aging father, tipped the political balance of power in Babylon's favor. He then forayed into Aram and Palestine as far as Egypt and made a minor raid on Jerusalem, taking Daniel and other members of the nobility to Babylonia. The foraging expedition was cut short by the news that Nebuchadnezzar's father had died. Nebuchadnezzar quickly returned to Babylon to be crowned king in 605 B.C.

Jehoahaz to Jehoiachin (609–597 B.C.)

Josiah's first son, Jehoahaz, initially succeeded his father, but Pharaoh Neco II deposed him, exiling him to Egypt, and put his brother, Jehoiakim, on the throne. From the very beginning of his reign, Jehoiakim and the prophet Jeremiah were adversaries. Early in Jehoiakim's reign, Jeremiah stood in the temple court and predicted that the temple would be destroyed if Judah did not repent of its sins. Neither Jehoiakim nor the priests and prophets who functioned at the temple appreciated these comments, and Jeremiah was tried for treason. Had it not been for

the intervention of the elder Ahikam, Jeremiah might have been
executed.

In 601 B.C. Nebuchadnezzar and Neco II met again in a battle
that turned out less decisively than Carchemish, and this may
have encouraged Jehoiakim to withhold tribute from the
Babylonian king. In any event, the Babylonians besieged Jerusalem in 598 B.C., and Jehoiakim died during the three-month
siege. His son Jehoiachin became king for the short duration of
the siege, after which the Babylonians put Zedekiah, another son
of Josiah, on the throne and exiled Jehoiachin to Babylonia.
Exiled with him were court officials, the queen mother, artisans
of Judah, and the prophet Ezekiel.

The Prophets of the Late Judean Kingdom

The fall of the Northern Kingdom and the constant national
threats by surrounding nations spawned a fervor of prophetic
activity during the Late Judean Kingdom. Prophets of this period
warned against the evils that felled the Northern Kingdom and
that threatened to do the same to Judah. Idolatry, injustice, and
immorality were some of the major indictments leveled against
the people of Judah, and destruction would surely befall them
unless they repented of their evil deeds. The following prophets'
oracles have been collected into books bearing their names and
have been included in the Hebrew canon of Scripture.

Isaiah began his public career in the year that King Uzziah
died (740 B.C.). Many of Isaiah's prophecies predicted the downfall of Judah and the subsequent exile to Babylonia, due to the
rampant idolatry and injustice in Judah. Isaiah's doomsday predictions, however, were difficult for the people to accept, since
they had grown accustomed to the prosperity and political stability that characterized the previous decades. Isaiah usually
addressed the people directly, although occasionally he gave
specific advice to the kings of Judah, including Hezekiah.

One contemporary of Isaiah was the prophet **Micah,** who prophesied from the small Judean town of Moresheth-gath. He began prophesying sometime before 722 B.C. and continued through the reigns of Jotham, Ahaz, and Hezekiah. Either Micah and Isaiah or their students must have had some knowledge of each other's oracles, or else they drew from a common source, since a few of their sayings are exactly the same.

Micah was chiefly concerned with the moral decay of Judah, the prevalence of false prophets, and the spiritual lethargy of the priests and the leaders due to the prosperity of the previous decades. Rather than calling the people to repentance, Micah subpoenaed them to plead their case before God, who was about to render judgment upon them for their deeds. God wanted the people to obey rather than to placate him with sacrifices. If they would refuse to do this, he would shake them out of their lethargy by exiling the leaders to Babylon, by reducing the temple to rubble, and by ending the visions of the false prophets.

Zephaniah prophesied during the reign of Josiah, to whom he may have been distantly related through Hezekiah. Religious syncretism and social injustice elicited Zephaniah's most scathing condemnations. Zephaniah warned that the "day of the Lord" was coming for the people of Judah and for the other nations, just as Amos had warned Israel decades earlier.

Perhaps the most passionate call for repentance came from the prophet **Jeremiah** during the rise of the Babylonian Empire, which was overtaking the waning Assyrian power. Aided by his gift for vivid symbolic action, Jeremiah pleaded with the people in Jerusalem to put an end to their empty religiosity and idolatry and turn to God in true obedience. As a warning of the coming judgment if Judah did not repent, Jeremiah wore a yoke around his neck to symbolize the impending exile to Babylonia. Also paired with Jeremiah's message of doom, however, was a promise of hope. God would return the people of Israel from exile and would establish a new covenant with them. This new covenant would be written on the people's hearts rather than on tablets of stone.

For the prophet **Nahum,** the capture of the Assyrian capital of Nineveh by the Babylonians underscored the justice of God. Nahum's oracles celebrate both the vengeance that will finally visit the wicked empire and the justice that will be shown to those who have suffered injustice at the hands of the Assyrians.

The prophet **Habakkuk** turned prophecy on its head by questioning God rather than the people. The violence and wickedness that pervaded Judah angered Habakkuk, and he questioned why God was not punishing the nation for its sins. Yet, almost as an unwanted answer to this question, Habakkuk could also foresee the rise of the Chaldeans and the possible demise of Judah. Habakkuk again questioned why God would use such an evil nation to punish Judah. God answered Habakkuk's questions, though not necessarily as the prophet would have liked. God would settle the question of justice in his own timing, both for Judah and for the Chaldeans. It is simply the responsibility of the righteous to live by faith.

Zedekiah and the Fall of Jerusalem
Three or four years into his reign, Zedekiah hosted ambassadors from Edom, Moab, Ammon, Tyre, and Sidon to discuss the prospects of rebellion against Babylon. The prophet Jeremiah, a political realist, relayed a message to the respective kings of these nations that they should submit to King Nebuchadnezzar. He knew they were no match for the power of Babylon, and he believed that God would lead Nebuchadnezzar from victory to victory until judgment was meted out upon these disobedient nations.

After nine years on the throne, Zedekiah rebelled against Nebuchadnezzar, and the Babylonians began a two-year siege of

Jerusalem. The Lachish Letters, a cache of messages written on pottery in the last years of Judah, provide insight into the country's attempt to withstand the Babylonian invasion. When the city fell in the summer of 586 B.C., the Babylonians burned the temple, ravaged the city, and exiled the nobility to Babylonia. The book of **Lamentations** recounts this grisly event in graphic Hebrew poetry. The fall of Jerusalem in 586 B.C. marked the end of the sovereign kingdom of Judah.

The Babylonians appointed a Judean named Gedaliah to act as governor over Palestine, but in only a few months he was assassinated. The Babylonians returned again in 581 B.C, taking another group of Judeans into Babylonian captivity.

An Edomite raid on Jerusalem after the Babylonians had captured it was most likely the occasion for the prophet **Obadiah's** condemnation of the Edomites, although there are scholars who date Obadiah earlier. Obadiah warned of the "day of the Lord" that would come upon all nations who rejoiced at the fall of Jerusalem.

. . . . .THE EXILE AND THE RESTORATION OF ISRAEL AND JUDAH

The Exile (588–538 B.C.)
In 605 B.C. the first Judeans were deported to Babylon to be educated and trained for administrative positions in Nebuchadnezzar's realm. In 597 B.C. a more substantial deportation occurred. Then in 586 B.C. yet another deportaton occurred after the fall of Jerusalem. Many Judeans who had anticipated the fall of Jerusalem had already fled to Egypt by this time. With Jerusalem in ruins, the history of the people of Israel shifts to the Exile in Babylon. Sources for this formative period are limited. The books of **Daniel** and **Ezekiel,** along with bits of information in Jeremiah and Psalm 137, comprise most of the information available.

Jeremiah's letter to the exiles around 594 B.C. and statements in Ezekiel suggest that the Jews had the freedom to build their own homes within their settlements, to plant gardens, to marry freely, and to meet for religious purposes, although there were isolated cases of religious discrimination. It appears that Jews could be elevated to significant positions of responsibility in the royal court. This policy continued during Persian rule after the Exile ended.

The Exile significantly and permanently impacted the culture and practices of the people of Israel. During this period the term *Jew* (a shortened form of *Judahite*) became the normal way of referring to the Israelites. Aramaic, a sister language to Hebrew, became the predominant language among the Jews. Eventually it became common practice in the synagogue for the Hebrew Scriptures to be translated into Aramaic after they were read. After the Exile a more urban, rather than rural, lifestyle became the norm.

Another significant by-product of the Exile was the rise of the synagogue movement throughout the world. The absence of the temple in regular worship forced Judaism to develop another means for cultivating prayer, study of the Scriptures, and fellowship. The local synagogue, a small gathering place for religious purposes, fulfilled this need. Synagogues became very popular among Jews throughout the world, and by the time of the first century A.D., almost every Palestinian town had one.

As the power and influence of Cyrus the Persian eclipsed the sovereignty of the neo-Babylonian dynasty, fortunes of the Jews in Babylon turned for the better. In order to placate his conquered subjects, Cyrus adopted a policy of religious and cultural tolerance, unlike the policies of Assyria and Babylonia. So, in 538 B.C., Cyrus issued a decree permitting the Jews in Babylonian exile (as well as other peoples) to return to their homeland

and begin reconstructing the temple that had been destroyed in 586 B.C.

The Return and Restoration of Israel and Judah

The books of **Ezra** and **Nehemiah** (originally written as one book) document the events of the return and reconstruction that followed the Babylonian exile. The story of **Esther** is set in this period. The books of **1 and 2 Chronicles** (also written as one book) were written sometime during this period in an effort to inform the displaced tribes of their true heritage, to give them a sense of purpose and direction as a people, and to give them hope for the future of their newly restored nation.

The restoration of the exiled Jews to their Judean homeland involved three phases: reconstructing the temple and reinstituting the priesthood and sacrifices, rebuilding the city of Jerusalem, and restoring the observance of Mosaic law.

The first phase of the return and restoration was led by the Persian-appointed governor, Sheshbazzar, possibly a descendent of the exiled King Jehoiachin. With the help of about fifty thousand Jews who had returned from Babylonia, the foundations of the new temple were laid. It is disputed whether Sheshbazzar is the same person as the governor Zerubbabel, grandson of Jehoiachin, who appears in the second phase of reconstruction. Nevertheless, the work of the first leader was interrupted by opposition from Judah's enemies.

The second phase began in the second year of Darius I (520 B.C.). At the encouragement of the prophet **Haggai** and the priest/prophet **Zechariah,** the central focus of this phase became the reconstruction of the temple and the reinstitution of the sacrifices. Under the governorship of Zerubbabel and the leadership of the high priest Jeshua, these goals were achieved, although the work again encountered strong opposition from Judah's enemies. At one point Judah's adversaries managed to halt the work, but a search of the royal archives produced the royal decree from Cyrus; the work resumed, and the temple was rededicated in 516 B.C.

Since **Joel,** like several other prophets, left no personal information aside from the name of his father, it is very difficult to determine the period of his ministry. The occasion of his prophecy was a devastating locust plague that also symbolized a future invasion awaiting the nation if it did not repent of its immoral deeds. Joel also promised restoration and hope, describing the future era as one in which all men and women would be prophets, sensitive and obedient to God's voice.

The narrative of Nehemiah skips from the completion of the temple (516 B.C.) to the arrival of Ezra (458 B.C.). The history of the Jews during this gap of fifty-eight years is fairly obscure, suggesting that few significant events occurred in this period.

The third phase of the return and reconstruction began with the arrivals of Ezra and Nehemiah. In the seventh year of King Artaxerxes's reign, the scribal priest Ezra arrived in Jerusalem to undertake certain religious reforms and then returned to Babylonia after the reforms were accomplished. With the permission of the Persian emperor, Nehemiah came to Jerusalem in 444 B.C. as governor of Judah and rebuilt the walls of Jerusalem. He also introduced economic reforms and reinstituted the sacrifices, which had been interrupted after Ezra's departure. As Nehemiah returned to Persia in 432 B.C., another period of decline began. Upon his return to Judah a few years later, Nehemiah found the Judeans intermarrying with foreigners. This and other abuses of Mosaic law, such as desecrating the Sabbath and withholding tithe from the Levites, became the primary focus of Nehemiah's work in Judah.

Two or three generations after the enthusiastic restoration of the temple, the priesthood had lost its integrity. Sacrificial abuses were common, and social decadence and religious apostasy were beginning to make postexilic Israel look much like preexilic Israel. It is probably to this situation that the prophet **Malachi** addressed his message of warning. The conclusion to his book mentions both Moses and Elijah, the exemplars of Law and Prophecy, illustrating the complementary nature of the two institutions in ancient Israel.

. . . . .EVENTS AFTER THE EXILE

During the period of the second temple, there were several significant events that shaped the culture of Palestine. The Persian Empire, which oversaw the reconstruction of Jerusalem, was eventually overthrown by Alexander the Great and his Greek empire. Alexander's empire was short-lived, however, and Palestine and Egypt came under the rule of Ptolemy I upon Alexander's death. The Ptolemies continued to rule Palestine until 198 B.C., when another Hellenistic empire, the Seleucids, gained control of Palestine.

In order to unify his vast Seleucid empire, Antiochus IV (Epiphanes) enforced a strict policy of Hellenization. This policy sought to suppress local customs and religions, so Judaism's most distinctive features, such as the Hebrew Scriptures and the rite of circumcision, came under the heaviest attack. Such persecution came to a climax when Antiochus dedicated the temple in Jerusalem to the Olympian god Zeus and sacrificed a pig (considered unclean by Jews) on the altar. These actions precipitated a revolt led by a priest named Mattathias and his sons. The revolt was successful, and the temple was retaken in 164 B.C. by Judas Maccabeus ("the hammer"). The festival of Hanukkah commemorates this event.

The Maccabean family ruled Judea until 63 B.C., when Pompey seized Palestine for the Romans. Governors directly oversaw Judea until Herod (later called "the Great") convinced the Roman senate to name him king. Herod was born an Idumean, not a Judean, and was governor of Galilee before his appointment as king of Judea. Upon Herod's death in 4 B.C., Palestine was divided up among his sons, Herod Archelaus, Herod Antipas, and Herod Philip. As each son died, his territory came under the control of Roman procurators. Herod Agrippa, grandson of Herod the Great, briefly ruled Judea from A.D. 41 to 44.

Eventually all of Palestine came under the direct control of the procurators, and the burdens they heaped upon the people became too much to bear. A massive Jewish revolt erupted in A.D. 66, but the destruction of the second temple in A.D. 70 sounded the death knell of the rebellion. The Romans quashed the final remnants of organized rebellion in A.D. 73 at the Dead Sea fortress of Masada.

. . . . .JUDAISM AFTER THE SECOND CENTURY B.C.

The dominant political and religious groups that were prevalent in first-century Palestine had their origins in the second century B.C. The Sadducees were a sect primarily associated with the priesthood. They were predominantly wealthy and aristocratic. They held only the first five books of the Hebrew Scriptures to be authoritative, and they did not believe in angels, demons, or the resurrection.

The sect known as the Pharisees probably arose out of a pro-Maccabean religious group called the Hasidim, who aided in the overthrow of the Seleucids. The Pharisees started out primarily as a political party, but by the first century A.D. they seem to have limited their concerns to religious matters. They were very intent upon observing every single law given by Moses, and they formed extensive traditions in order to ensure that Moses' laws were carried out. The strict code of the Pharisees was complemented by their insistence upon separation from those who were more lax in their religious practices.

The Essenes, who have received an enormous amount of attention in recent years due to the discovery of the Dead Sea Scrolls, were another religious sect who probably also arose out of the

Hasidim. The Essenes were also concerned with ritual purity, but they were less involved in mainstream society, preferring instead to live in separate communities and to influence others by example. The Essene community at Qumran, near the Dead Sea, understood itself as the true Israel, and they prepared themselves for the day when God himself would come to restore Israel.

There were also various political-activist groups, such as the Zealots and the Sicarii, who worked for the overthrow of the Roman government in Palestine. While it is still uncertain whether the Zealots themselves were an actual organized group at the time of Jesus Christ, it is clear that there were several groups of this nature already in existence. Eventually these groups helped initiate the Jewish revolt of A.D. 66–73.

The prevailing worldview among first-century Palestinian Jews and Christians was apocalypticism. This worldview developed during the very difficult era of the Seleucid empire, when Jews were being persecuted for what they considered righteous actions. This view understood the earth as being under the control of the evil one, and the only way it would be restored was through the miraculous intervention of God himself. When this happened, the faithful righteous would be rewarded, and the evil oppressors would be judged. Various works of literature arose out of this worldview, and many of them contained similar features, including visions, riddles, supernatural encounters, and speeches about the end times and the coming of the Messiah. This worldview attempted to make theological sense of the harsh oppression that plagued Jews and Christians during these times. Most of the first-century revolts against the Romans were grounded in apocalyptic thought.

. . . . .THE LIFE AND MINISTRY OF JESUS CHRIST

Before studying the New Testament books, it is essential to become familiar with the life of Jesus Christ, since his life and actions are the touchstone for every book in the New Testament canon. The most significant, and almost sole, sources for reconstructing an outline of the life of Jesus Christ are the four Gospels of the New Testament (**Matthew, Mark, Luke,** and **John**). These four works, presented in the form of historical narrative, arrange the actions of Jesus as a definite progression from his birth to his crucifixion and resurrection. Each of the Gospels presents this progression in a unique fashion, and all four Gospels concentrate on the last three years of Jesus' life. These last three years were especially significant, since they form the period of Jesus' public ministry. Furthermore, all four Gospels devote several chapters to the last week of Jesus' life because it was in this final week that Jesus was first hailed as king, but then was betrayed, arrested, tried, and crucified. Each of the Gospels concludes with Jesus' resurrection from the dead. The Gospel of Luke adds that Jesus was then taken up into heaven.

Matthew, Mark, and Luke (the synoptic Gospels) present a fairly uniform account of Jesus' travels. According to these Gospels, Jesus journeys from Galilee to Jerusalem only once (except in Luke, where he also visits the city as a young boy). This arrangement intensifies the drama surrounding the events of Jesus' final week in Jerusalem. During this momentous last week, Jesus is first hailed as king in a triumphal entry and then is condemned to death by crucifixion. The Gospel of John, however, uses a different framework for arranging the events of Jesus' life. In this fourth Gospel, Jesus travels to Jerusalem several times, predicting from the very first visit that he would be killed by the Jewish leaders there. Thereafter, Jesus is increasingly persecuted every time he visits Jerusalem.

The following summary of the life and ministry of Jesus draws upon all four Gospels to reconstruct an outline of events. It is important to remember that the Gospel writers were not so concerned with the order of the various events as they were with the significance and meaning of each episode.

Jesus' Birth

John is the only Gospel to mention Jesus' existence before birth. John attests that Jesus existed even before the creation of the world. As the Son of God, Jesus Christ was "the Word" (the very expression of God), and he was also "God" (John 1:1). He was with God the Father from the very beginning and collaborated with him in the creation of the world (John 1:2-3). Then the Son of God became human; John describes it as "the Word became human and lived here on earth among us" (John 1:14). The beginning of John's Gospel makes it clear that he was not just recording the events of any ordinary human being; he was recounting the life and actions of the God-man himself.

Matthew and Luke provide some of the details of how Jesus' birth happened. In Matthew's account, the coming of Jesus is announced beforehand to Joseph through dreams; in Luke's account, it is announced by an angel who appears to Mary. Both Gospels are careful to point out that Jesus' birth was recognized as unique. Both Gospels affirm that Mary conceived Jesus by the Holy Spirit rather than by Joseph, to whom she was engaged. Both Gospels recall visits by strangers who also recognize Jesus' uniqueness. These visits also set the stage for the writers to emphasize the universal nature of Jesus' message.

Both Matthew and Luke link their birth accounts to genealogies. It is difficult to harmonize these genealogies since they appear to be drawn from different sources, but the purpose in both cases is to show that Jesus was legally descended from Abraham and David.

Life in Nazareth

The events of Jesus Christ's formative years are given only a few lines in the Gospels. Details are given of only one incident from his childhood: the discussion the twelve-year-old Jesus had with the religious teachers in the temple (Luke 2). This event foreshadows a key feature in Jesus' later ministry: constant debate with the Jewish religious leaders over matters of Law and Scripture. This event also presents Jesus as being acutely aware of a divine mission even at the age of twelve.

Aside from this event, not much else is said of Jesus' formative years except that he was obedient to his parents and grew in wisdom and favor. It is assumed that during his years at Nazareth Jesus learned the carpenter's trade from his adoptive father, Joseph, and became the village carpenter after Joseph's death, since he is called "the carpenter" and "the carpenter's son" in the Gospels.

The Preaching of John the Baptist

John the Baptist, the cousin of Jesus, began a national repentance movement in the wilderness sometime before Jesus' public ministry. John called the nation to be baptized as a sign of their repentance. John's methods resembled those of the Israelite prophets before the Exile. He was most likely an ascetic, since he and his followers regularly fasted, and John was described as wearing rugged clothing and eating locusts. His austere appearance and uncompromising moral challenge effectively prepared the way for the public appearance of Jesus. The importance of John's groundwork among the people can hardly be underestimated in regard to Jesus' later ministry. The Gospel writers are careful to note, however, that John was only a forerunner of Jesus. John's significance was not to eclipse the importance of Jesus and his ministry, but, rather, to set the stage for it.

The Baptism of Jesus

At age thirty, Jesus enters the public arena after his baptism by John the Baptist. All four Gospels place this event at the very beginning of Jesus' public life and emphasize the significance of this event as a divine commission. After Jesus is baptized, God declares his approval of his beloved Son, and the Holy Spirit descends upon him. This divine anointing is reminiscent of the anointing of the first several kings of Israel and Judah. Like these kings, Jesus was being divinely appointed to begin his new ministry to Israel. With his divine commission, Jesus begins his public ministry, calling the people to "turn from [their] sins and turn to God, because the Kingdom of Heaven is near."

The Temptation of Jesus

Jesus' baptism revealed the divine calling of his mission. The temptation that followed shows the nature of the environment in which he is to minister. Immediately after his baptism, Jesus is led by the Holy Spirit into the wilderness, where he fasts and is tempted by Satan. Confrontation with adverse spiritual forces characterizes Jesus' whole ministry. On this occasion, Satan confronts Jesus with the temptation to choose a path other than the one God has designed for him. In each instance, Jesus appeals to Scripture to overcome the temptation, and he refuses to take matters into his own hands. This encounter establishes from the beginning that Jesus has come to do the will of God, regardless of his own personal fate. This story also portrays Jesus as a genuine human being who, like everyone else, is subject to temptation, yet he does not yield to it.

The Early Ministry of Jesus in Judea and Samaria

Only John's Gospel tells of the work of Jesus in Judea following his baptism. In Judea Jesus calls the first disciples, John and Andrew. These first two disciples would soon be joined by three others: Peter, Philip, and Nathanael. These five formed the nucleus of the band of Jesus' followers who came to be known as the Twelve. Jesus' initial calling of these five was followed later by a more definite call to leave their occupations as fishermen in order to "fish for people" (Matthew 4; Mark 4; Luke 5).

John records that soon after Jesus began his ministry in Judea he returned to the region of Galilee, where he attended a wedding. At this wedding Jesus' mother, Mary, prompted him to turn water into wine after the wine had run out. This event is important in John's account because he notes it as the first of the signs, or miracles, that Jesus performed after leaving Judea (John 2).

Within this initial period John places two incidents that occurred at Jerusalem. The first is the cleansing of the temple (John 2:13-16). The synoptic Gospels place this event just before Jesus' trial at the end of his career, but John places it at this early stage. Angered by the money changers who were turning the temple into a marketplace instead of a house of prayer, Jesus drives them out and overturns their tables. By this display of concern for true worship, Jesus revealed the purpose of much of his ministry. The synoptic Gospels imply that this action sparked the hostility of his opponents, who would eventually kill him.

John's other incident in Jerusalem is the meeting between Jesus and Nicodemus (John 3). John uses this opportunity for Jesus to explain about being spiritually "born again" (or "born from above").

John's narrative then moves from Judea to Samaria, where Jesus encounters a Samaritan woman at a well (John 4). Pious Jews did not associate with Samaritans, since they were viewed as a mixed race and did not worship at the temple. Jesus uses the woman's physical thirst to point to her deeper spiritual thirst. Jesus then explains that he can quench this thirst because he is the one sent from God to restore true worship. The woman becomes a believer in him and spreads the news throughout Samaria.

The Period of the Galilean Ministry

After spending some time in Judea with John the Baptist, it appears that Jesus must have returned to Galilee to begin the first major phase of his ministry. Most of the information regarding Jesus' Galilean ministry is found in the synoptic Gospels. This period encompasses the events surrounding the choosing of the Twelve, the various controversies and debates with religious leaders, Jesus' miracles, and Jesus' work in northern Galilee. While the synoptic Gospels concentrate exclusively on the events in Galilee, John's account indicates that Jesus also made some visits to Jerusalem during this period.

THE CALLING OF THE DISCIPLES   In each of the synoptic Gospels there is an account of a call to four disciples to leave their fishing boats and accompany Jesus. Apparently they had already met Jesus and must have had some idea of what was involved in following him. Jesus did not appoint them at this time to be apostles, but this call was an important step toward the establishment of the twelve apostles. Another significant call came to Levi, also known as Matthew. He would certainly have been despised by his Jewish contemporaries because of his profession. But his inclusion in the special circle of Jesus' disciples shows the variety of backgrounds from which these individuals were chosen. The synoptic Gospels list the names of the twelve who eventually became apostles (Matthew 10:2-4; Mark 3:16-19; Luke 6:14-16).

The synoptic Gospels detail the instructions Jesus gave to his disciples before sending them to minister in Israel. These instructions show Jesus' concern for preparing his disciples for their future work. They were to proclaim the kingdom of God as Jesus did, but they were not to suppose that all would respond to their message. Jesus also warns them about coming hostility and persecution.

Throughout the rest of the Gospels, Jesus teaches his disciples about a wide range of topics. Most of his teaching took the form of parables; these were short stories, often about everyday events, that carried a deeper, allegorical meaning. Parables became a key feature of Jesus' ministry.

VARIOUS CONTROVERSIES AND MIRACLES   Shortly after Jesus began his public ministry, he arrived in his hometown of Nazareth and taught in the synagogue there. The people refused to believe his message, however, since he had grown up among them and was known simply as the town carpenter.

The rest of Jesus' public ministry was filled with controversies, healings, teachings, and remarkable miracles. Jesus did not hesitate to confront his contemporaries on issues involving moral or religious questions. He outraged many religious leaders by his association with the outcasts of society. Jesus often attended dinners where there were tax collectors and prostitutes, and he was willing to touch lepers and other outcasts. Through these actions, Jesus emphasized God's concern for the rejected members of society.

On several occasions, Jesus became involved in debates over the observance of the Sabbath. These controversies usually stemmed from healings that he performed on the Sabbath. Some leaders seemed to regard ritual observance of the Sabbath as of greater importance than compassionate concern for people. Jesus often deliberately performed healings to bring this issue to light. Many leaders became even more incensed because Jesus claimed that this was the work of God. Jesus' attention to the heart contrasted sharply with the widespread concern for ritual obedience.

The rising opposition to Jesus' miracles did not deter him from performing other healings. But when Jesus healed a demon-possessed man who was blind and mute, the Pharisees accused him of casting out demons by Beelzebul, the prince of the demons. Jesus argued that he was acting by the power of the Holy Spirit and that to deny this power was blasphemy. Other notable miracles were the healing of the Roman centurion's servant and the raising of a widow's dead son at Nain.

John records two visits to Jerusalem by Jesus during this period. These are difficult to date, but they probably occurred during the early period of his ministry. He attended the Feast of Tabernacles and the Feast of Dedication, or Hanukkah (John 7–10). At these times Jesus taught in the temple area and entered into dialogue with the religious leaders. The chief priests became alarmed at his presence and sent officers to arrest him. Instead of arresting him, however, John writes that the officers themselves were captivated by Jesus' teachings. More discussions with religious leaders followed. Jesus described himself as the Good Shepherd of his flock, angering many listeners, who picked up stones to kill him.

One of Jesus' miracles described by all four evangelists is the feeding of the five thousand. This event reveals Jesus' concern for the physical needs of people and marked a high point of Jesus' popularity among the people.

NORTHERN GALILEE   Jesus spent a brief time in the region of Tyre and Sidon, where he performed more healings but made it clear that his primary mission was to the people of Israel. He then moved on to Caesarea Philippi.

The discussion at Caesarea Philippi was clearly the turning point in Jesus' ministry, because it was here that Jesus asked his disciples: "Who do people say that I am?" Peter responded, "You are the Messiah, the Son of the living God." Jesus then instructed his disciples not to tell anyone the secret of his true identity.

In the synoptic Gospels, this revelation of Jesus' identity is reinforced by the Transfiguration. In the presence of Peter, James, and John, Jesus is momentarily transformed from an earthly form to a heavenly form, revealing his true nature to his disciples.

After the Transfiguration, Jesus makes two predictions concerning his approaching death. These announcements completely perplex the disciples. Peter tries to convince Jesus not to go to Jerusalem if this will be his fate, but Jesus rebukes him. Jesus is resolved to fulfill the plans of God.

The Closing Period

Luke devotes more than half his Gospel to the events between the trip to Jerusalem and Jesus' death and resurrection. In this section Luke introduces a great deal of material that is not included in the other Gospels. Parables and teachings about the kingdom of God form much of this material.

ON THE WAY TO JERUSALEM   As Jesus travels toward Jerusalem, he is aware that he will not be with the disciples much longer, and so he prepares them for the future. He teaches them about prayer, about the Father's care for them, and about his return in the future.

Along the way, Jesus visits both Jericho and Bethany. At Jericho he heals Bartimaeus and has dinner with Zacchaeus, who then reforms his crooked practices as a tax collector. Bethany was the home of Mary and Martha and their brother, Lazarus, whom Jesus had raised from the dead (John 11). It is here that Mary anoints Jesus with costly ointment. The Gospels defend her expression of love for him by noting that this anointing prepared Jesus for his burial.

JESUS' FINAL WEEK IN JERUSALEM   All four Gospels describe the Triumphal Entry of Jesus into Jerusalem. By this time many people had heard of Jesus and his miracles, and rumors were beginning to circulate that he might be the expected Messiah. While there were several different theories of what the Messiah would be like, most of them envisioned a triumphant, conquering hero who would free Israel from political oppression. This almost certainly contributed to the excitement of Jesus' grand entrance.

As Jesus rode into the city on a donkey, multitudes greeted him with praises, acclaiming him as their king. This welcome no doubt excited the disciples, who still were unclear as to Jesus' ultimate destiny.

The synoptic Gospels place the cleansing of the temple as the first main event following Jesus' entry into the city. The audacity of Jesus' actions outrages the religious leaders, and they begin to plot his demise.

Nearing his final hour, Jesus takes the opportunity to instruct his disciples about future events, especially concerning the end of the world. He reiterates the certainty of his return and mentions various signs that will precede his coming (Matthew 24; Mark 13; Luke 21). Jesus challenges the disciples to be watchful and diligent.

On the evening before Jesus was crucified, he arranged to celebrate the Passover with his disciples. The Passover meal celebrated the Israelites' deliverance from oppression in Egypt, and there were several symbolic pieces of food to be eaten and cups of wine to be drunk. As Jesus celebrated this meal with his disciples, he wished to give them a means by which the significance of his approaching death could be remembered. So he modified the ritual meal to be done in remembrance of him. Bread came to symbolize his body, and wine represented his blood, which would be poured out to seal a new covenant with his followers. This has since been called the Lord's Supper, or Holy Communion, or the Eucharist, which is still celebrated by Christians in remembrance of Jesus' death.

John's Gospel also records the story of Jesus' washing the feet of his disciples as an example of humility (John 13). He impresses upon them the importance of serving others in humility. Jesus then follows this display of humility with a series of teachings. It is here that Jesus promises to send the Holy Spirit, who will come to them after Jesus has gone.

JESUS' BETRAYAL AND ARREST   There is a sense in which the whole gospel story has been working up to a climax of rejection. The various outbursts of popular support are over, and Jesus' opposition is determined to eliminate the threat that he poses to their established system. John's Gospel refers to this approaching climax as "his hour" (John 13:1).

From the upper room, where the Last Supper was eaten, Jesus and his disciples went straight to Gethsemane, where he prayed to his Father with deep intensity and agony. He prayed that, if it was possible, he might be delivered from the suffering that awaited him. Nevertheless, he continued to submit to the Father's will. The three disciples with him fell asleep, while Judas Iscariot led a band of soldiers into Gethsemane to arrest Jesus. Judas was also one of the Twelve, but he betrayed his master for the price of a slave. Greeting him with a kiss, Judas disclosed Jesus' identity to the soldiers, and they immediately came forward to arrest him. After a brief discussion, Jesus was taken into custody while the disciples fled.

JESUS' TRIAL   There appears to have been a great deal of confusion about who held jurisdiction over Jesus' trial, and he was shuffled from place to place. The leaders questioned him about various aspects of his teaching until, finally, they settled on the charge of blasphemy for claiming to be the Messiah. Meanwhile, Peter and another disciple watched from a distance, never allowing themselves to be associated with Jesus. Peter even directly denied his connection with Jesus three times.

Eventually Jesus was handed over to Pilate, the Roman governor of Judea. Pilate appears to have been reluctant to charge Jesus with anything, since this seemed to him to be a religious dispute. The Jewish leaders pressed him, however, and charged that Jesus claimed to be a king. Pilate finally acquiesced to their demands, but he washed his hands of responsibility for Jesus' death by giving the people a choice between Jesus and Barabbas, a bandit. The people chose to crucify Jesus.

JESUS' CRUCIFIXION   Jesus was led away to be crucified the morning after his trial. Crucifixion was a standard method of execution throughout the Roman Empire. Jesus was taken to a place called "Skull Hill" outside Jerusalem. The synoptic Gospels note that a man from northern Africa named Simon was forced to carry Jesus' cross. After Jesus' hands and feet were nailed to the cross, a sign detailing the charges against him was placed above him, and he was placed on display for all passersby to witness. His charges read, "This is the King of the Jews." Two bandits were also crucified with him.

Though the torturous process of crucifixion normally lasted several days for a victim, Jesus died within a few hours. John notes that as the soldiers came by to break the legs of the victims, thereby speeding up the execution, they noticed that Jesus had already died, and so they thrust a spear into his side to make certain that he was dead.

The Gospels are careful to recount Jesus' crucifixion as a fulfillment of Scripture. Many of the events surrounding Jesus' crucifixion were matched with corresponding Old Testament passages in order to show believers that this was all part of God's plan from the very beginning. A few examples include: the disciples' desertion of Jesus (Matthew 26:31 from Zechariah 13:7), the casting of lots for Jesus' tunic (John 19:24 from Psalm 22:18), and the soldiers' decision to refrain from breaking Jesus' legs (John 19:36 from Psalm 34:20).

Jesus' Burial, Resurrection, and Ascension
Jesus' body was placed in a newly hewn tomb that belonged to Joseph of Arimathea. Jesus' mother and Mary Magdalene

watched as a large stone was placed over the opening to the tomb. Roman guards were stationed at the tomb to ensure that no one came to steal the body away.

On the third day after Jesus' crucifixion, Jesus was raised from the dead by the power of the Holy Spirit. The Gospels tell of an angel who came down from heaven and rolled back the stone. The guards became terrified and passed out. When Jesus' mother and Mary Magdalene came to finish preparing the body with spices, they found the tomb empty. They went back and told the disciples, who were in hiding. The disciples did not believe the women at first, but then they went and saw for themselves that the body was not in the tomb.

Later Jesus appeared to the disciples, assuring them of his resurrection and their hope. Many of these appearances occurred in Galilee, where the disciples returned after Jesus' death. Jesus then promised that he would send the Holy Spirit, and he commissioned the disciples to go throughout the whole world, making followers of Jesus Christ.

Luke adds that after forty days Jesus was then taken up into heaven, where he was seated at the right hand of God. This means that Jesus has been given the highest position of authority under God.

. . . . .THE BIRTH AND SPREAD OF THE CHRISTIAN CHURCH

The only New Testament work documenting the birth and spread of the church is the book of **Acts.** This book is a continuation of Luke's Gospel, and so the primary emphases of these two books are very similar.

The Coming of the Holy Spirit at Pentecost

Before Jesus ascended to heaven, he instructed his disciples (now called apostles) to wait until the Holy Spirit descended upon them, and then they would preach the Good News of the

Resurrection throughout the earth. In the meantime they chose another disciple, Matthias, to replace Judas Iscariot, who had committed suicide after betraying Jesus.

The Jewish festival of weeks, or Pentecost, was held fifty days after Passover, and many Jews from throughout the Roman Empire had come to Jerusalem to celebrate. It was during this time that the Holy Spirit descended upon the apostles. As the apostles were filled with the Holy Spirit, they began speaking in various languages. Peter then stood up in front of a large crowd and began to preach that Jesus was the Messiah and that God had raised him from the dead. Nearly three thousand people responded to Peter's message, and they committed themselves to the apostles' teaching, to fellowship with other believers, and to the observance of the Lord's Supper. The first believers formed a sort of voluntary commune in which members sold their possessions and distributed the proceeds among the other members according to their needs. This marked the birth of the Christian church.

The Early Work of the Apostles

For the first several years, the Christian church had the immense task of defining itself and its structure. The twelve apostles oversaw much of this early work and helped establish the foundation upon which the church would be built.

Many early Christians did not completely break from Jewish religious practices. Acts 2:46 mentions that the believers met often in the temple. Throughout the first century, many Christians still attended the synagogue as well as the church. The book of James even uses the Greek word for *synagogue* rather than *church* as the place where believers would come together.

The earliest churches were located in Palestine. Likewise, the earliest converts to Christianity were Jews. Eventually, however, the gospel (Good News) of Jesus Christ would be extended to

the entire Gentile world, predominantly through the work of
Paul of Tarsus.

The Life and Ministry of the Apostle Paul

Paul of Tarsus is perhaps the most significant figure in the expansion of the church into the Gentile world. Highly educated in
both Greek and Hebrew literature and zealous for preserving his
Jewish faith, Paul (also called Saul) first entered Christian history as a persecutor of Christians. After a conversion experience
on the road to Damascus, however, he became a driving force in
the spread of Christianity, especially among the Gentiles. His letters to various churches form a significant portion of the New
Testament corpus. The following summarizes the life and ministry of this influential apostle.

PAUL'S BACKGROUND   Paul was born in Tarsus of Cilicia
(Asia Minor) to a family of Pharisees from the tribe of Benjamin
(Philippians 3:5). His parents named him Saul after the first king
of Israel, who was also a Benjaminite, but Acts 13:9 notes that
he was "also known as Paul." After Saul's conversion to Christianity in Acts, he is always referred to as "Paul," and this is the
name he used in all his letters to the churches.

Paul's native city of Tarsus was a center of commerce and
learning that embraced Hellenistic thinking and Roman politics.
It served as the capital of the Roman province of Cilicia. In 171
B.C. Jews were brought to Tarsus to promote business in the
region. It is possible that Paul's ancestors arrived in Tarsus at
this time and were granted Roman citizenship. Paul inherited
Roman citizenship from his father, and this proved invaluable in
his travels with the gospel. Paul may have had several brothers
and sisters, although only one sister is ever mentioned in the
New Testament (Acts 23:16).

Paul was educated in the Law and the Prophets and became
well versed in Hebrew, Aramaic, Greek, and probably Latin as

well. Although born in the city of Tarsus, Paul apparently spent his youth in Jerusalem under the training of Gamaliel (Acts 22:3). It is not clear when Paul was first brought to Jerusalem, but it is likely he began his formal rabbinical studies sometime after he turned thirteen. His teacher, Gamaliel, was the grandson of Hillel, who founded a very influential Pharisaic school. Hillel's teachings can be found throughout the Talmud. Gamaliel once persuaded the Sanhedrin to spare the lives of Peter and the apostles (Acts 5:33-40). It was almost certainly during this period of study that Paul began to advance in Judaism beyond many Jews of his own age and became extremely zealous for the traditions of Judaism (Galatians 1:14). Paul eventually became a tentmaker (Acts 18:3), or perhaps a leatherworker. He may have learned this trade from his father, or he may have selected it as a means of self-support, as did many in rabbinical training.

THE PERSECUTOR   While Paul was studying Jewish law in Jerusalem, Jesus was probably working as a carpenter in Nazareth. Years later, Jesus entered into public ministry and gathered together his disciples, who would one day be Paul's fellow workers in the gospel. In the meantime, however, Paul rose to a level of significant influence among the religious leaders in Jerusalem.

The sudden explosion of Christianity among Jews alarmed religious leaders in Jerusalem. Tensions increased between the new followers of Jesus and the other Jewish leaders. In time the situation came to a climax when Stephen, a follower of Jesus, angered members of a synagogue in Jerusalem (Acts 6:9-10). They accused him of blasphemy before the Sanhedrin. After Stephen's lengthy and eloquent defense, they dragged him out of the city, where he was stoned to death. The killing of this first martyr launched a wave of persecution against the followers of Jesus, and Paul was given special orders to hunt them down and arrest them.

CONVERSION AND CALLING   Paul obtained letters from the high priest to arrest believers in the Damascan synagogues and bring them to Jerusalem for trial (Acts 9:1-2). As Paul traveled to Damascus, however, he had an encounter that would forever change his life. At the outskirts of the city a light from heaven, brighter than the midday sun, shone around Paul and his entourage. Everyone fell to the ground, and Paul heard the voice of Jesus confront him and instruct him to go into the city to await further instructions. Temporarily blinded, Paul was led into Damascus, where a disciple named Ananias prayed over him. Paul received his sight again and became a follower of Jesus as well. The Christian community forgave Paul for persecuting the church, baptized him, and helped him through the bewildering event of his conversion (Acts 9:10-22).

After a short time with the church in Damascus, Paul received death threats from Jews to whom he preached the message of Jesus, but he was protected by the believers and escaped.

PREPARATION   After Paul's experiences in Damascus, he began a several-year period of preparation, much of which was spent in the desert of Arabia. Following this, Paul returned to Damascus and then visited the apostle Peter in Jerusalem for fifteen days (Galatians 1:17-18).

At first the disciples in Jerusalem were afraid of Paul, uncertain whether he was truly a disciple of Jesus (Acts 9:26). After he was endorsed by a leader named Barnabas, however, he was accepted by the believers in Jerusalem. Paul preached in Jerusalem, but when his life was threatened once again, the believers sent him away to Tarsus (Acts 9:29-30; Galatians 1:21).

The end of Paul's preparation came when Barnabas went to Tarsus to look for him and to bring him to Antioch (Acts 11:25-26). By this time Paul had been living in Cilicia for ten years, boldly proclaiming the message of Jesus.

SENT OUT FROM ANTIOCH   The church in Antioch was formed by believers who fled persecution in Jerusalem after the death of Stephen (Acts 11:19). At first the scattered believers shared the gospel only with Jews. In Antioch, however, the gospel was opened to the Gentiles as well, and many became believers. It is fitting that Paul, the apostle to the Gentiles (Acts 22:21; Romans 11:13), should appear in Antioch to formally begin his ministry.

Barnabas and Paul stayed with the church in Antioch for a year. It was here that the new name *Christian* was coined to distinguish the followers of Jesus from other Gentiles and Jews (Acts 11:26). Hearing of a famine in Judea, the Christians in Antioch determined to send relief to the believers in Judea. Barnabas and Paul delivered the church's gift, and the potency of the gospel among the Gentiles was clearly displayed to the Jewish churches. Afterward, Barnabas and Paul returned to Antioch with John Mark, Barnabas's cousin.

Beginning from the Day of Pentecost, the work in the gospel had been fairly incidental. Contacts were made in homes, the marketplace, the streets, synagogues, highways, etc. But in Antioch, a determined effort was made to evangelize a specific section of the Roman Empire (Acts 13:1-3). The church designated Barnabas and Paul for this work. With the prayers and encouragement of the church and with John Mark as their assistant, Barnabas and Paul set sail for Cyprus.

TRAVEL WITH BARNABAS   Arriving in Salamis, Paul and Barnabas traveled the length of the island of Cyprus, preaching in synagogues along the way (Acts 13:5-6). When they reached Paphos, the Roman proconsul, Sergius Paulus, wanted to hear the word of God. A magician named Elymas Bar-Jesus tried to prevent the proconsul from believing but was stricken with temporary blindness at Paul's command.

Paul and his companions then set sail from Paphos and arrived in Perga of Pamphylia. John Mark deserted them there and returned to his home in Jerusalem (Acts 13:13). This apparently caused some dissension between Paul, Barnabas, and John Mark, but Paul and Mark were later reconciled (Colossians 4:10; 2 Timothy 4:11).

Paul's travels with the gospel continued throughout the mainland of Asia Minor, specifically in the Roman provinces of Galatia, Pamphylia, Pisidia, and Lycaonia. Paul and Barnabas were asked to speak at the synagogue of Antioch in Pisidia (Acts 13:15). After they delivered their message, they were invited to speak the next week. Acts records that "almost the entire city turned out to hear them preach the word of the Lord" (Acts 13:44). The jealousy that was stirred up among Jews who opposed Paul's message precipitated his decisive turn to the Gentiles. Many Gentiles in Antioch believed the gospel and spread it throughout the region, but Paul and Barnabas were forced out and went to Iconium in Lycaonia (Acts 13:48-51).

Paul and Barnabas experienced the same success and opposition in Iconium that they had in Antioch (Acts 14:1), and the apostles fled the threat of a stoning. In Lystra Paul healed a man who had been crippled since birth (Acts 14:8-10). The citizens began worshiping Paul and Barnabas as the Roman gods Mercury and Jupiter, who were believed to have visited this region. Paul had to convince the people that he and Barnabas were merely mortals who served the living God.

It was in Lystra that Paul received his first serious persecution for the gospel. Many Jews there stoned him, dragged him out of the city, and left him for dead (Acts 14:19). Paul's disciples came to his aid, Paul recovered, and then he moved on to Derbe with Barnabas. After making many disciples in Derbe, the apostles retraced their steps through Lystra, Iconium, and Pisidian Antioch, strengthening and encouraging the new believers and appointing elders in each church (Acts 14:21-23). Arriving again in Perga, they sailed back to Syrian Antioch, where they reported to the church the news that God had extended the gospel to the Gentiles.

THE COUNCIL OF JERUSALEM   In Syrian Antioch, many Jews opposed Paul's message of grace, which did not require Gentiles to keep the law of Moses. These Jews began teaching the Christians there that they must be circumcised according to Mosaic law. This caused a heated debate between Paul and the Jewish leaders. It is very possible that Paul's letter to the **Galatians** may have been written around this time (ca. A.D. 49), although some scholars date this letter later (ca. A.D. 56). Paul wrote this bold letter to counteract the legalistic influence of many Jews in Galatia and to show that the grace provided by Jesus Christ was sufficient and could be obtained by faith alone. The epistle of **James** was probably written around this time as well. While it is debated whether this letter from Jesus' brother is actually antithetical to Paul's letter to the Galatians, it is clear that it represents a very Jewish perspective regarding Christianity.

In order to settle the controversy regarding Mosaic law, the church in Antioch sent Paul, Barnabas, and others to Jerusalem to meet with the apostles and elders there (Acts 15:2). Along the way they spread the news of Gentile conversions. This brought great joy to the believers, but such joy was not shared by some in Jerusalem. In the first meeting of the Jerusalem Council, some argued that the Gentiles should be "required to follow the law of Moses" (Acts 15:5). Peter countered this by insisting that "we are all saved the same way, by the special favor of the Lord Jesus" (Acts 15:11). After long debate, James, the brother of Jesus, reached the decision that they should not trouble those Gentiles who were turning to God (Acts 15:19). A few basic restrictions were placed upon the Gentile believers, but the

Mosaic law, as a whole, was not enforced. An official letter was drawn up to be sent to the churches, informing them of the decision. This was a significant decision for the Christian church, and the news was received joyfully by the church in Antioch.

FURTHER TRAVEL   Paul desired to revisit the churches that he and Barnabas had visited earlier. He wanted to see how they were doing (Acts 15:36). Barnabas wanted to take John Mark with them, but Paul refused since he had deserted them during their earlier journey (Acts 13:13). A sharp disagreement over this matter ended Barnabas's association with Paul. Silas, a leader among the brothers in Jerusalem, accompanied Paul as he set out by land through Syria and Cilicia, strengthening the churches there (Acts 15:40-41).

Beginning from Derbe in Galatia, Paul and Silas revisited the churches that Paul had helped establish earlier. While in Lystra they were joined by Timothy (Acts 16:1-3). The apostles delivered the letter from the Jerusalem Council to these young churches.

It is likely that Ephesus, a major city in the Roman province of Asia, was Paul's primary objective for advancing the gospel, but he was told by the Holy Spirit not to speak the word in Asia (Acts 16:6). They attempted to turn north and enter the region of Bithynia, "but again the Spirit of Jesus did not let them go" (Acts 16:7). So Paul and his party were forced to continue straight westward to Troas, on the Aegean Sea, where Luke probably joined them. After experiencing a vision in which he was called out of Asia into Macedonia (Acts 16:8-9), Paul and his party immediately crossed by boat into Europe, where they carried the gospel to Philippi, Thessalonica, Berea, Athens, and Corinth.

Philippi was a Roman colony and military outpost where there were few Jews, so Paul went to a place by the river where the local Jews gathered to pray. He spoke to some women there, notably Lydia, who believed and was baptized, along with her whole household (Acts 16:12-15). Paul also cast a spirit of divination out of a girl there, and, as a result, he and Silas were arrested, flogged, and jailed (Acts 16:16-24). Paul eventually disclosed his Roman citizenship and was released, but he was asked to leave the city. From Philippi, Paul traveled to Thessalonica.

Some Jews at Thessalonica became jealous of Paul's success in communicating the gospel, and they gathered a mob to search for the apostles. They complained to the city authorities that the men who had "turned the rest of the world upside down" had come to disturb their city, and they accused the apostles of professing "allegiance to another king [besides Caesar], Jesus" (Acts 17:5-7).

Paul and Silas quickly left Thessalonica by night and arrived in Berea, whose citizens eagerly and thoughtfully received the gospel (Acts 17:10-12). Some Thessalonian Jews, however, had followed Paul to Berea to incite the crowds. The believers then sent Paul away to Athens, while Silas and Timothy stayed behind.

The Athenians quickly labeled Paul a babbler but let him air his views before the Areopagus. Paul's speech there displayed a broad knowledge of Greco-Roman philosophy, poetry, sculpture, architecture, and religion. He made reference to an altar to "an Unknown God," but his speech was cut short when he mentioned the Resurrection (Acts 17:22-32). Paul's words delighted the minds of many but influenced the wills of few. When he arrived in Corinth, Paul determined not to proclaim the mystery of God in lofty or wise words, so that the believers' faith would not rest on human wisdom but on the power of God (1 Corinthians 2:1-5).

In Corinth Paul met Aquila and Priscilla (or Prisca), Roman Jews with whom he lived and worked as a tentmaker. Eventually these two would become prominent among the churches (Romans 16:3; 1 Corinthians 16:19; 2 Timothy 4:19). Paul stayed in Corinth eighteen months in A.D. 50–51, establishing and strengthening the church there. It was most likely during this time that Paul wrote two letters (**1** and **2 Thessalonians**) to the church in Thessalonica, encouraging them to lead holy, industrious lives in the hope of the second coming of Jesus Christ.

Accompanied by Priscilla and Aquila, Paul set sail from Corinth to Syria. Along the way he stopped at Ephesus, leaving Priscilla and Aquila there as he then sailed on to Caesarea. After briefly visiting Jerusalem, Paul returned to Antioch, where he remained for a while (Acts 18:18-23). He departed alone from Antioch, going from place to place in Galatia and Phrygia and strengthening the disciples. Eventually he arrived back in Ephesus (Acts 18:23; 19:1).

LABOR IN THE GOSPEL   At Ephesus a man from Alexandria named Apollos had been preaching eloquently about "the way of the Lord," though he had only been made a disciple of John the Baptist. Priscilla and Acquila took him aside and explained more fully who Jesus was. After that he began to preach that Jesus was the Messiah. Paul also instructed some disciples of John the Baptist (Acts 19:1-7), explaining to them the significance of Jesus and the work of the Holy Spirit. He then spent three months preaching at the local synagogue until members of the congregation "spoke against the Way."

Paul led John's disciples to the neutral ground of Tyrannus's school (Acts 19:9), where Jews and Greeks were free to come. He continued his work there for two years, and "people throughout the province of Asia—both Jews and Greeks—heard the Lord's message" (Acts 19:10).

In Ephesus Paul enjoyed an effective ministry bolstered by extraordinary miracles, a public burning of sorcery books, and the assistance from officials of the province of Asia (Acts 19:11-41). But there were many adversaries, especially among the artisans associated with the temple of Diana. Paul's ministry had hurt their trade to the extent that they incited a riot (Acts 19:23-41). Paul had intended to stay in Ephesus until Pentecost (1 Corinthians 16:8), but this tumult seems to have hastened his departure.

During Paul's stay in Ephesus, someone from Corinth sent word that there were divisions in the Corinthian church (1 Corinthians 1:10-13). This report generated a flurry of letters and travels. Paul wrote a letter to Corinth, but this letter is now lost, unless it is part of 2 Corinthians (1 Corinthians 5:9). The church in Corinth wrote back (1 Corinthians 7:1) and sent messengers to Paul (1 Corinthians 16:17). Paul sent Timothy to them (1 Corinthians 4:17; 16:10). Paul then wrote what is now known as **1 Corinthians** around A.D. 53 and sent it by Titus, who was to meet him in Troas to report the results (2 Corinthians 2:12-13).

After his hurried exit from Ephesus, Paul found an open door for the gospel in Troas, but he so longed to hear from Corinth that he pushed on into Macedonia (2 Corinthians 2:12-13). There he was finally comforted by news from Titus (2 Corinthians 7:5-7) and rejoiced over the Corinthians' repentance and renewed enthusiasm (2 Corinthians 7:8-16). From Macedonia Paul wrote what is now known as **2 Corinthians** (A.D. 54), toured northwest to proclaim the Good News of Christ in Illyricum (Romans 15:19), and then turned south for Achaia and his third visit to Corinth (Acts 19:21; 20:1-3; 2 Corinthians 13:1).

During a three-month winter stay in Corinth (A.D. 55–56), Paul wrote the letter to the **Romans,** which solidified his explanation of the gospel. Paul had many personal friends in Rome (Romans 16) and had long intended to visit there (Romans 1:9-15). But first he wanted to deliver relief funds from the Gentile churches to the Jerusalem church (Romans 15:25-26; 1 Corinthians 16:1). He then planned to visit Rome on his way to Spain.

THE ARREST IN JERUSALEM   As Paul traveled from Corinth, he was repeatedly warned of danger awaiting him in Jerusalem, but he insisted on continuing. He carried the collection for Jerusalem, journeying swiftly in order to reach Jerusalem by Pentecost (Acts 20:16). They proceeded by land from Achaia, through Macedonia, and on to Philippi in time for Passover (spring A.D. 56). Crossing by sea to Troas, they visited the believers there and then sailed to Miletus through the archipelago of the eastern Aegean Sea (Acts 20:7-16). From Miletus Paul sent for the elders of Ephesus and passionately warned them of false teachers who would soon come (Acts 20:17-38).

Paul and his companions then set sail to Cos, to Rhodes, and then to Patara, where they changed ships for Phoenicia (Acts 21:1-2). A straight course to Tyre brought them within sight of Cyprus (Acts 21:3). The disciples in Tyre again warned Paul not to go on to Jerusalem, but he pressed on to Caesarea, where he and his company stayed with Philip, who had formerly served with the martyred Stephen. In Caesarea, Paul still would not be persuaded by an especially dramatic prophecy of his coming arrest (Acts 21:10-14).

In Jerusalem Paul's entourage stayed with Mnason and were warmly welcomed by the other Christians there (Acts 21:15-17). James and the church elders praised God when they heard what had been accomplished among the Gentiles (Acts 21:18-20). They thankfully received the collection from the churches but warned Paul of his bad reputation among the thousands of Jewish Christians in Jerusalem. They urged him to convince the believers that he did not encourage forsaking the Mosaic customs (Acts 21:20-24). In order to correct this misunderstanding, Paul agreed to join in a sacred Jewish vow ceremony.

While Paul's vow may have satisfied the Christians, there were still many Jews who despised him. Jews from Asia, visiting Jerusalem for the Pentecost feast (A.D. 57), incited a riot against Paul (Acts 21:27-29), and the whole city became involved. The crowd dragged Paul out of the temple and tried to kill him, but he was rescued by Roman soldiers. Paul made a futile attempt to explain himself to the crowd, and the soldiers brought him into the barracks. The soldiers prepared to flog Paul, but at the last minute he revealed his inherited Roman citizenship. At this the Roman tribune became afraid to deal with Paul until he had learned more of the charges against him (Acts 22:25-30).

Paul was brought before a council of Jewish leaders. He began his defense with heated words but changed his strategy when he noticed many Pharisees at the council. He intentionally created bitter dissension between the council members by insisting that he was being tried for belief in the resurrection of the dead. The uproar between the Pharisees and the Sadducees over this issue caused the tribune to take Paul back into the barracks. There the Lord appeared to him and encouraged him, promising that he would present his defense in Rome (Acts 23:10-11).

In the meantime, more than forty Jews vowed not to eat or drink until they had killed Paul (Acts 23:12-15). With the help of Paul's nephew, however, the conspiracy was exposed. For safety, Paul was taken from Jerusalem to Caesarea under guard of 470 soldiers and handed over to the custody of Felix, the governor (Acts 23:16-35). Over a period of two years in Caesarea, Paul was brought before Felix; his successor, Festus; and King Agrippa. Festus suggested that Paul be returned to Jerusalem for trial, but Paul knew the murderous intent of his accusers and appealed his case to Caesar himself (Acts 25:9-12).

VOYAGE AND STAY IN ROME   In order to plead his case before Caesar, Paul and his companions, Aristarchus and Luke, were taken to Rome by way of a perilous sea voyage (A.D. 58, Acts 27:1–28:16). Luke's account of the journey from Caesarea to Rome is a treasure of information on ancient ships, navigation, and seamanship. Luke traces the voyage stage by stage through every crisis, with a change of ship at Myra, a delay at Fair Havens on Crete, and a shipwreck on Malta.

In the spring of A.D. 59, they arrived at Puteoli, Italy, and made their way to Rome, welcomed by believers along the Appian Way (Acts 28:13-15). Paul was allowed to live in a house of his own under Roman guard (Acts 28:16, 30). There he received the local Jewish leaders and taught about Jesus without interference. Paul most likely penned several letters to churches during this period (A.D. 60–62), including those known as the Prison Epistles. Paul's letter to the **Ephesians** (though it was most likely sent to each of the Asian churches) was probably the first. This epistle discusses the great mystery of Christ and the church. The second and third epistles were sent to the **Colossians** and **Philemon.** The personal letter to Philemon was sent along with the letter to the Colossian church, since Philemon was a member there. The letter to the Colossians asserts the superiority of Christ over all other religions and philosophies, while the letter to Philemon is Paul's appeal on behalf of a runaway slave named Onesimus. The letter to the **Philippians** was sent last, expressing Paul's aspirations to know Christ and anticipating release from prison.

FINAL YEARS AND MARTYRDOM   Apparently Paul made quite an impression on the Roman guard in his home, and several members of Caesar's household became believers—perhaps through Paul's ministry (Philippians 4:22). It is possible that a good report about Paul was given to Caesar as a result, and Paul was released from prison around A.D. 62. Romans 15:28 indicates that Paul intended to visit Rome on his way to Spain after he delivered the collection to Jerusalem. His arrest and imprisonment in Jerusalem altered these plans. Paul may still have gone to Spain after his release, which came a couple years before the burning of Rome on July 19, A.D. 64. Returning east, Paul left Titus in Crete (Titus 1:5) and traveled through Miletus, south of Ephesus, where he left Trophimus (2 Timothy 4:20). Traveling toward Macedonia, Paul visited Timothy in Ephesus (1 Timothy 1:3). Along the way Paul left his cloak and books with Carpus in Troas (2 Timothy 4:13). He may have intended to return there later for his possessions.

From Macedonia Paul wrote **1 Timothy,** a loving letter of instruction to his young coworker in the gospel (A.D. 63–64). Paul decided to spend the winter in Nicopolis (Titus 3:12), northwest of Corinth on the Adriatic Sea, but was still in Macedonia when he wrote to **Titus.** This letter is similar to 1 Timothy, yet with a somewhat harsher tone. This letter also gives a final glimpse of the eloquent and zealous Apollos (Titus 3:13), who is still in association with Paul ten or more years after his first appearance in Ephesus (Acts 18:24).

From here Paul's path is obscure. He may have wintered in Nicopolis, but he did not return to Troas for his winter cloak (2 Timothy 4:13). At some point he was arrested by the Romans, because he spent a winter in Rome's Mamertine Prison, suffering from the cold in a rock cell. Paul may have been anticipating the coming winter when he requested that Timothy bring his cloak (2 Timothy 4:13, 21). During this imprisonment Paul wrote **2 Timothy** (A.D. 66–67). Paul wrote this letter because he was anxious to see his disciple before his own death. In case Timothy did not arrive in time, however, Paul felt it necessary to warn him of the heresies that were infecting the churches.

While it is possible that the charges against Paul were related to the burning of Rome, it is not certain. By this time it was "illegal" to be a Christian, since it was no longer protected by Roman law as a sect of Judaism. These circumstances made life very dangerous for Paul at this time. Many of his workers deserted him (2 Timothy 4:16), including all the Christians who had come from Asia (2 Timothy 1:15) and Demas (2 Timothy 4:10). Only Luke, the author of Luke and Acts, was with him when he wrote his second letter to Timothy (2 Timothy 4:11). Faithful believers

still in hiding in Rome were also in contact with the apostle
(2 Timothy 1:16; 4:19, 21). Paul instructed Timothy to come to
him in Rome and to bring Mark with him (2 Timothy 4:11).
Apparently Timothy did come and was imprisoned (Hebrews
13:23). Paul's request for the books and parchments (2 Timothy
4:13) discloses that he was reading and studying to the end.

The apostle Paul had two hearings before Emperor Nero. At
his first defense, Paul not only pleaded his own cause but also
that of the gospel, still longing that all the Gentiles would hear
its message (2 Timothy 4:17). Perhaps no decision was made,
and thus he was rescued from "certain death" (2 Timothy 4:17).
Though he knew he would soon die, Paul was not afraid; he was
assured that the Lord would reward him at the end of time
(2 Timothy 4:8). Finally, the apostle blessed all believers: "May
the Lord be with your spirit. Grace be with you all" (2 Timothy
4:22). After this, the New Testament is silent regarding Paul.

Nothing is known of Paul's second hearing except that it
resulted in the sentence of capital punishment. The events surrounding Paul's death are unrecorded. Nero died in the summer
of A.D. 68, so Paul was probably executed before that date. As a
Roman citizen, Paul must have been spared the torture that often
attended such a sentence. Tradition holds that Paul was decapi-
tated by the sword of an imperial headsman on the Ostian Road
just outside of Rome and was buried nearby. This fulfilled Paul's
desire "to go and be with Christ" (Philippians 1:23).

Later Work of the Apostles
The other apostles continued to spread the gospel throughout the
Roman Empire after Paul's death. Peter apparently established a
ministry in Rome, where he wrote **1 Peter** (ca. A.D. 63). This letter was written to several churches throughout Asia to console
those who were experiencing hardship for the sake of the gospel.
He encouraged them to live godly lives among unbelievers in

order to present a living example of the gospel of Jesus Christ. The epistle of **2 Peter** is traditionally thought to have been written late in Peter's life. This letter warns against false teachers and encourages the readers to grow in their faith. Tradition holds that Peter was eventually martyred around A.D. 66.

The letter to the **Hebrews** was most likely written by a close associate of Paul. It is doubtful that Paul himself penned it, based upon differences in the structure and style of the book. This book was written to admonish and instruct a group of believers who were apparently having second thoughts about the superiority of Christianity over Judaism. The epistle of **Jude** was written to defend the truth against false teaching that led to complete lawlessness. It is ascribed to the brother of Jesus, who was also the brother of James.

The apostle John also carried on a significant ministry well beyond Paul's lifetime. As an elder to the church in Ephesus, John wrote **1, 2,** and **3 John** to nearby churches in Asia in order to warn them against false teaching. The Gospel of **John** was probably written some time after these letters. The book of **Revelation** is also attributed to the apostle John. This apocalyptic book draws upon imagery from the Old Testament to encourage Christians who were being persecuted for the gospel.

. . . . .CHRONOLOGY OF BIBLICAL EVENTS

      1447 B.C. The Exodus (early date)
      1270 B.C. The Exodus (late date)
      1400 B.C. The Conquest (early date)
      1230 B.C. The Conquest (late date)
      1010 B.C. David Becomes King of Israel and Judah
       931 B.C. The Beginning of the Divided Kingdom
       722 B.C. The Fall of Samaria (Northern Kingdom)
       597 B.C. The First Babylonian Deportation

586 B.C. The Fall of Jerusalem

538 B.C. Cyrus Conquers Babylon; End of Babylonian Exile

516 B.C. Completion of the Second Temple

457 B.C. Ezra Arrives in Jerusalem

444 B.C. Nehemiah Arrives in Jerusalem

6/5 B.C. Birth of Jesus Christ

A.D. 6/7 Young Jesus in the Temple

A.D. 26 John the Baptist Begins His Ministry

A.D. 26/27 Jesus Christ Is Baptized, Begins His Ministry

A.D. 30 Jesus Christ Is Crucified and Resurrected

A.D. 30 Coming of the Holy Spirit at Pentecost

A.D. 34/35 Paul's Conversion

A.D. 44 James the Apostle Is Martyred

A.D. 46–48 Paul's First Missionary Journey

A.D. 49/50 Jerusalem Council

A.D. 50–52 Paul's Second Missionary Journey

A.D. 53–57 Paul's Third Missionary Journey

A.D. 60–62 Paul's Imprisonment in Rome

A.D. 67 Paul's Second Imprisonment

A.D. 65–67 Peter Martyred

A.D. 68 Paul Martyred

A.D. 90–95 John Exiled

Book Summaries

. . . . .THE PENTATEUCH

The Pentateuch, also called the Law or the *Torah,* contains
the first five books of the Old Testament. These books, Genesis,
Exodus, Leviticus, Numbers, and Deuteronomy, detail the origins of the Israelite nation, beginning with Creation, following
through the Egyptian sojourn and the Exodus, and ending with
the nation at the edge of the Promised Land of Canaan. Moses
has traditionally been regarded as the author of the Pentateuch,
and writers of other Old Testament books assume his authorship
as well. Over the centuries, however, this traditional view has
been seriously challenged. Many current theories endorse some
version of the "Documentary Hypothesis," which understands
the existing Pentateuch as the last in a series of editions made by
various writers over time.

Depite the arguments raised about the books' authorship, it is
clear that the Pentateuch was written within a consistent theological framework, which gives unity to the entire collection of
books. The divine promise to Abraham, that is, the promise of
posterity, of land, and of a relationship with God, forms the theological backbone of the Pentateuch. This promise drives the

actions and movements of the characters throughout the Pentateuch, and it is repeated to each successive generation. This
coherent theme throughout the Pentateuch gives strong support
that it was assembled by a single writer.

GENESIS   Genesis is generally divided into two major
sections, primeval history (chapters 1–11) and patriarchal history
(chapters 12–50). It is important to note that this division has
been made by later readers based on the content of the two
sections. The writer of Genesis, however, divided the book by
interjecting the genealogical formula, "these are the generations
of . . . ," which occurs eleven times throughout the book.

Genesis appropriately opens with the creation of the world
and humanity. The first chapter presents a very structured
account of God's creative acts, organized into six days. The first
three days involve forming light and dark and the earth and the
seas, while the second three days involve filling these creations.
The order of the second three days matches the order of the first
three and places the appropriate creatures in their respective habi-
tats. Finally, on the seventh day, God rests from the work he has
done.

Creation stories in Near Eastern culture usually established
who, as the creator of all things, should be worshiped as the
supreme God. The Hebrew creation story, in addition to establishing the God of the Hebrews as supreme, sets people apart
from the rest of creation by noting that they have been created
in the image of God and have been given God's breath or soul.
They are then placed over creation and commanded to take care
of it.

The story of the fall of Adam and Eve explains the existence
of evil in the world. The first couple disobeys God's command
not to eat of the tree of the knowledge of good and evil, and, as a
result, the whole earth is cursed. God denies the couple access to

the tree of life, and so death becomes inevitable for the human race.

As the human race multiplies in number, it also multiplies in wickedness, and so God decides to eliminate his creation and start over. There are other flood stories that have been found throughout Mesopotamia, and most of them contain numerous parallels to the biblical account: Creation becomes alienated from God; judgment is pronounced on the human race; one righteous man and his family are forewarned of the coming flood; an ark is built according to divinely given plans; the man, his family, and his animals are saved; various birds are released to determine whether the waters have subsided; and the survivor's offering is received with favor. In the Hebrew account, God then establishes a covenant with Noah, the survivor, promising never again to destroy his creation by flood.

Genesis then traces the various ethnic groups and peoples back to Noah's three sons, and the story of the Tower of Babel accounts for the different languages of the human race. The primeval history of Genesis then comes to a close by tracing the genealogy of Shem through ten generations to arrive at Abraham and his descendants, the dominant characters for the rest of the book.

The rest of Genesis follows the exploits of Abraham, Isaac, Jacob, and Joseph, who are the patriarchs, or forefathers, of the nation of Israel. The patriarchal section begins with Abram (later named Abraham) living in southern Mesopotamia. God calls him to leave Mesopotamia and travel to Canaan. While passing through Canaan, God vows to bless Abram and his descendants, who will be as numerous as the stars in the heavens, and to give them the land of Canaan. This was the first of many occasions that God revealed this promise to Abram and his descendants.

Despite the advanced ages of Sarai and Abram, God promises them a son and gives them Isaac to fulfill his promises to them.

God also changes the name of Abram to Abraham, meaning "father of many," and the name of Sarai to Sarah. God then tests the depth of Abraham's faith by telling him to sacrifice Isaac, the heir to the promise. Abraham is willing, but at the last moment God provides a ram instead.

Following the death of Abraham, the narrative shifts to Isaac and his travels, which resemble his father's wanderings. God reiterates his promise of land and descendants to Isaac, whose wife Rebekah gives birth to twin sons, Jacob and Esau. A key event in the lives of these two sons occurs when Esau, the older brother, sells his birthright to Jacob, thereby conferring upon him the family name and most of the inheritance. This birthright is finally secured at the end of Isaac's life, when Jacob tricks his father into giving him the blessing that should have gone to the oldest son, Esau. By this, Jacob becomes the heir to the promise of his father and grandfather.

Jacob eventually marries two wives, and, through them and their servant girls, twelve sons are born that become the ancestors of the twelve tribes of Israel. Jacob's name is changed to Israel, meaning "one who struggles with God," and God repeats his promise of posterity and land to Jacob.

The final character in the patriarchal section is Joseph, the favorite son of Jacob. Joseph's favored status with his father and his dreams of superiority anger his brothers, who sell him into slavery to some travelers on their way to Egypt. In Egypt Joseph rises to a position of authority among the slaves of Potiphar, the captain of Pharaoh's bodyguard. Joseph is then falsely accused of attempted rape and jailed. In prison he interprets the dreams of some fellow inmates, one of whom is subsequently reinstated to his position in Pharaoh's court. Later, when Pharaoh becomes troubled by a dream, Joseph's name is given as an able interpreter. Joseph interprets the dream, predicting a famine in the years to come, and is put in charge of storing up grain for the disaster. During the famine, Joseph's brothers come down from Canaan to buy grain from the new overseer of the storehouses. Joseph hides his true identify from them until he manages to assemble all his brothers before him. He then reveals himself to them, assuring them of his forgiveness and asking them to send for his father, Jacob. The book of Genesis draws to a close as Jacob and his family settle in Egypt.

Creation of the World and of Humanity (1:1–2:25)
Fall of Adam and Eve and Curse of the World (3:1–7:24)
Renewal of the Earth and Humanity (8:1–11:32)
History of Abraham (12:1–25:18)
History of Isaac (25:19–28:9)
History of Jacob (28:10–36:43)
History of Joseph (37:1–50:26)

EXODUS   Exodus, which means "a going forth," is so called because its primary focus is on Israel's departure from Egypt and the incidents that surrounded this memorable event. The book of Exodus recounts Israel's liberation from Egypt and the unique covenant that was then established between God and Israel. This covenant fulfilled one facet of the divine promise that runs throughout the Pentateuch—the promise of a special relationship with God.

The narrative of Exodus picks up where Genesis ends. Jacob and his sons are in Egypt enjoying very favorable conditions, and the family begins to grow into a sizeable people. After an undisclosed amount of time, a new king comes to power in Egypt and does not know of Joseph and his beneficent deeds toward his host nation. This new king becomes concerned for the security of his nation and begins conscripting Hebrews into his labor force in order to maintain tighter control over them. Eventually the king's policy toward the Hebrews escalates to partial genocide. An infant named Moses is spared, however, through the efforts of his mother and an unwitting daughter of the king himself.

Moses is raised in the court of the king, but he must flee the country when he kills a man in defense of a Hebrew. After many years of shepherding in the Sinai region, God instructs Moses through a divinely burning bush that he must return to Egypt to rescue the Hebrews. Moses returns and confronts the new Pharaoh, insisting that he permit the Hebrews to worship their God in the desert. Pharaoh refuses, setting in motion ten plagues from God upon the Egyptian nation. The tenth plague, the death of every firstborn male who is not specially protected by a blood sacrifice, finally breaks Pharaoh's resolve, and the Hebrews are allowed to leave Egypt in what is called the Exodus.

After the Hebrews' miraculous crossing of the "Sea of Reeds" to escape the pursuing Egyptians, Moses leads the nation to Mount Sinai, where the people prepare to meet with God. On Mount Sinai God establishes a covenant with the nation of Israel, which includes the Ten Commandments as part of the treaty.

The word *covenant* applies to the union of two parties in a legal relationship. In many respects, God's covenant with Israel in the book of Exodus follows the characteristics of treaties made between nations of that time period. Such treaties consistently contained a number of characteristics: (1) a *preamble* introducing the ruling king; (2) a *historical prologue* reflecting on the good things done for the vassal by the king; (3) a list of *covenant stipulations* or conditions to be obeyed by the vassal; (4) the writing and depositing of an official *document* naming the stipulations of the covenant, and a *public reading* of it; (5) a naming of *witnesses* to the treaty; (6) an *oath* accompanied by a *sacrificial ceremony*; and (7) a listing of *curses* if the covenant stipulations are not followed and *blessings* if they are obeyed.

In the case of Israel's covenant with God, Israel is the vassal nation, and God is the ruling king. God freely chose to perform benevolent deeds for Israel and was under no obligation or compulsion to do so. Therefore God, as the sovereign king, gives the terms of the treaty, the Ten Commandments, and the vassal, Israel, has no choice but to obey. Punishment will result if the conditions are not met, but the blessing of God's presence will be the fruit of obedience.

God then gives instructions for building the tabernacle. This sanctuary symbolizes God's presence among the nation of Israel and houses the symbols of the covenant. While Moses is on Mount Sinai receiving God's instructions, however, the people rebel and worship a golden calf, and Moses is forced to intercede for them. Punishment and repentance then follow, the covenant is renewed, and the tabernacle and the tent of meeting are constructed. The book of Exodus concludes with God's glory filling the tabernacle, symbolizing that God's covenant with the people of Israel has been sealed. The promise of a special relationship with Abraham and his descendants has been fulfilled.

> Oppression of Israel in Egypt (1:1-22)
> Moses and the Ten Plagues (2:1–12:36)
> Israel in the Wilderness (12:37–18:27)
> Israel at Mount Sinai (19:1–34:35)
> The Construction of the Tabernacle (35:1–40:38)

LEVITICUS The book of Leviticus was named for its emphasis upon priestly, or levitical, laws. Leviticus should be studied in conjunction with the book of Exodus, since it is most likely a continuation of the covenant stipulations given in Exodus. The last chapters of Leviticus contain the *blessings* and *curses* sections of the covenant formula, which are missing from the covenant sections of Exodus. The primary emphasis of Leviticus is the holiness of the nation. Its laws protect moral and ceremonial purity, detailing the removal of defilement and the maintenance of holiness. Cultic regulations dominate Leviticus, suggesting that ritual holiness was of primary importance to the nation of Israel. Social relationships within the covenant community receive instructions as well, however, and can be summed up by the statement, "Love your neighbor as yourself" (Leviticus 19:18).

Sacrifice was considered the normal ritual for removing defilement, and Leviticus endorses this ritual. It is important to note, however, that the attitude of the one giving the sacrifice was of primary concern, rather than the ritual itself.

Leviticus formally establishes the priesthood, who are to function as mediators between God and humans, chiefly by offering sacrifices. Priests also instructed in matters of law. Leviticus designates the holy days to be observed on the sacred calendar. On these days Israel was to remember what God had done for them and give him praise. Israel would be reminded throughout the year that they were God's chosen people.

> Instructions for Offerings (1–7)
> Initiation and Consecration of the Priesthood (8–10)
> Clean and Unclean Things Distinguished (11–15)
> Day of Atonement (16)
> Social and Ceremonial Prescriptions (17–25)
> Covenant Blessings and Curses (26)
> Instructions Concerning Vows and Offerings (27)

NUMBERS   In Hebrew, the book of Numbers is named "In the Wilderness," which are the opening words of the book. Indeed, Numbers is about what happened to Israel in the wilderness from Mount Sinai until the entrance into the Transjordan.

The English title comes from a census that is taken three times in the book.

The combination of priestly material, historical narrative, and census information in this single book has perplexed some scholars. Understood in its wider Pentateuchal context, however, Numbers is the narrative link between the arrival at Sinai and the entrance into the Promised Land. As a result, the theme of march and conquest runs throughout the book. In the course of the journey, several other themes become evident, including God's presence in the marches, God's providence for Israel, and God's patience with the people.

As the stay at Mount Sinai draws to a close, God directs Moses to take a census of the men who could participate in the upcoming conquest of the Promised Land. The extremely large number of eligible draftees has led scholars to translate the word *elef* as "military unit" or "clan" rather than "one thousand." A second census is made to determine the number of Levites available for tabernacle duty. Special instructions are also given for dismantling and transporting the sanctuary.

With some difficulties along the way, the Israelites move north to the oasis called Kadesh-barnea near the southern border of Canaan. From this base camp Moses dispatches twelve spies to obtain intelligence information before beginning the conquest. All twelve spies agree that the land is extremely lush, but ten report that the cities are too well fortified and the residents too strong to conquer. Only Joshua and Caleb believe that the covenant promises concerning the land ensure that God will give Canaan to Israel. The majority of the people side with the ten spies and consider a return to Egypt. Because of their unbelief, God does not lead the people to the immediate conquest, and the Israelites are condemned to wander in the wilderness for forty years. During their years of wandering, the Israelites suffer many difficulties, yet God continues to provide for their needs.

The later chapters of Numbers recount Israel's circuitous march from Kadesh-barnea and the difficulties they encounter by moving into position at the northeast corner of the Dead Sea. One episode of particular interest involves the Moabite king, Balak, who instructs a prophet named Balaam to curse the Israelite army and halt its advance.

The last chapters of Numbers detail various preparations that were made as Israel was about to enter Canaan. For example, another census of men available for war is taken, Joshua is designated as Moses' successor, and the Transjordan is alloted to the tribes of Gad and Reuben and to half of the tribe of Manasseh.

> Preparations for the Journey to the Promised Land
>   (1:1–10:10)
> First Approach to the Promised Land (10:11–12:16)
> The Wilderness Wanderings (13:1–19:22)
> The Conquest of Transjordan (20:1–22:1)
> The Events in the Plains of Moab (22:2–36:13)

DEUTERONOMY Deuteronomy, or "second law," was written as a collection of parting speeches by Moses as he was about to turn the control of Israel over to Joshua. In these speeches, Moses makes commentary on the Law, reviewing and even adapting some of its stipulations. He looks back in history to recall how God had indeed been faithful to Israel since their departure from Egypt. Moses then looks forward, reminding Israel of their special relationship with God as his chosen people. Deuteronomy includes a verse that has become the creed of Israel, "Hear, O Israel! The Lord is our God, the Lord alone. And you must love the Lord your God with all your heart, all your soul, and all your strength" (6:4-5). The book of Deuteronomy closes with the death and burial of Moses.

Deuteronomy's many parallels with Exodus have intrigued

scholars as to the actual date of the book's composition. Many scholars hold the book to be a product of the so-called Deuteronomic School that actively supported King Josiah and his reforms. Conversely, it is argued that Deuteronomy contains the same treaty form as Exodus, and thus conforms to treaty patterns of the last half of the second millennium B.C. rather than to patterns of the first millennium B.C. One requirement of the early treaties is the periodic reading of the treaty by those who are subjects of the sovereign king. Deuteronomy could be the copy of the treaty that would have been read before the people as Israel renewed its covenant with God.

The writer of Deuteronomy repeatedly refers to his work as "this book of the law" or as some variation thereof, as does the writer of the following book of Joshua. The book of Deuteronomy was the standard used by the writers of 1 and 2 Kings to evaluate the different kings of Israel and Judah. Clearly Deuteronomy was a significant book in the religious, social, and political life of ancient Israel.

Preamble (1:1-5)
Historical Prologue (1:6–3:29)
Covenant Stipulations (4:1–26:19)
Blessings and Curses (27:1–30:20)
Witnesses and Reading of the Text (31:1–32:52)
Final Blessings of Moses (33:1–34:12)

. . . . .HISTORY

The historical books include Joshua, Judges, Ruth, 1 and 2 Samuel, 1 and 2 Kings, 1 and 2 Chronicles, Ezra, Nehemiah, and Esther. These books contain Israel's history from the time of the conquest of Canaan to the period of Babylonian exile and the rebuilding of the temple. Joshua, Judges, 1 and 2 Samuel, and 1 and 2 Kings compose the collection known as the Former

Prophets in the Hebrew arrangement of books, and the remaining historical books belong to the Writings. The Former Prophets form a complete history of Israel from the conquest of Canaan to the Babylonian captivity. These books were written earlier than the other historical books included among the Writings. The Writings belong to the period of reconstruction after the Babylonian exile. These books were written to further the historical record (Ezra-Nehemiah, Esther) or to reinterpret history from a later perspective (the Chronicles).

The historical books are far more than bare history. The Former Prophets and the Writings are also prophetic and theological. They record history that reveals the character of God and the nature of humankind. They highlight God's acts of grace and redemption. The historical books, like the books of the Latter Prophets, were written to exhort readers to stop sinning and return to obeying God.

JOSHUA Jewish tradition regards Moses' successor, Joshua, as the author of the book which bears his name. Although the book is written from the standpoint of an eyewitness, the book itself makes no assertions as to its author. Early critical investigators divided the book into several strands of sources and placed its final compilation in the seventh century B.C., according it little historical value. Less negative appraisals acknowledge that Joshua may indeed have been compiled by a later editor, but the editor may have used accurate earlier sources.

Clearly the central focus of the book of Joshua is the conquest and subsequent division of the Promised Land into tribal allotments. The author also develops the theological theme of God's faithfulness to the covenant promises, first to the patriarchs and then to Moses and Israel. This theme culminates at the end of the book as Joshua reminds the people of God's faithfulness and rallies everyone together at Shechem to renew the covenant.

The narrative begins on the east side of the Jordan River with Joshua succeeding Moses as leader and commander of the Israelites. Joshua begins coordinating the conquest by sending two men across the Jordan River to spy out the point of entry into the land. The spies find Jericho in a state of tension because the Israelite camp is visible from Jericho and details of their former victories have preceded them. When the spies return with a favorable report, Joshua moves the people to the Jordan River. As the priests prepare to cross the river with the ark of the covenant, the waters upstream are suddenly blocked, and the people walk across on dry land.

Once across the Jordan River, Israel gathers at a place near Jericho, called Gilgal, where they celebrate Passover. Israel then conquers Jericho after God miraculously destroys the walls surrounding the city. Israel moves on to climb three thousand feet out of the Jordan Valley and into the hill country. A small party advances on the city of Ai, which guards access to Palestine's central plateau area, but they are routed by the Canaanites. Afterward, Joshua learns that a man named Achan has disobeyed God's command not to loot the city of Jericho. The Israelites were supposed to destroy the city completely because its fall had been dedicated to God. Achan is taken away and stoned, and a more elaborate attack on Ai proves successful as a result. With a foothold into the hill country established, Joshua then takes Israel north to Mount Gerizim and Mount Ebal, where the new nation is solemnly reminded of its covenant responsibilities.

The various city states of Canaan react in different ways to the arrival of Israel. When Ai falls, the people of Gibeon know they are next in line should Joshua turn south, and so they trick Joshua into a peace treaty. Several of the cities farther to the south realize that the city of Gibeon guards the route into their hill country, and so they lay siege to Gibeon in order to tighten up their mutual defense. When the Gibeonites appeal to Joshua for help, he and his troops begin marching toward the besieged city. Joshua routs the armies that surround Gibeon and sends them fleeing southwest out of the hill country. God miraculously lengthens the day for Joshua to ensure complete victory.

The rest of the conquest is summarized in the remaining chapters of Joshua. A casual reading of Joshua could give the impression that the conquest happens quickly, but actually seven years elapse during this period. A careful reading of the text also reveals that much of the land is not taken. Many city-states remain in Canaanite hands, and some of the cities that Joshua does conquer are resettled by Canaanites and subsequently have to be recaptured. Nevertheless, the conquest can be judged a success. The remaining city-states are isolated, and no federation is able to contest Israel's hold on the land.

After the conquest is completed, the tabernacle is moved to Shiloh in the central hill country. A very careful process is then followed to determine how the boundary lines should be drawn for the various tribes. The tribe of Levi is not given a specific area like the other tribes. Instead, they are deeded forty-eight cities throughout the other tribes so that they, as the religious leaders, can permeate the life of Israel. Six of these forty-eight cities are specified as cities of refuge where alleged murderers would be sheltered until their cases are decided. The covenant renewal at Shechem, followed by Joshua's death, brings the book to a close.

Entrance to Canaan (1–5)
Conquest of Canaan (6–12)
Dividing the Land (13–21)
Settlement and Establishment (22–24)

JUDGES The term *judges* refers to leaders who arose periodically in Israel from the time of Joshua's death until the establishment of the monarchy. These temporary leaders functioned primarily in a military role rather than in a judicial capacity, and their influence tended to be fairly localized. The Hebrew word for judge, *shophet,* would probably be more accurately translated as "avenger" or "deliverer."

Jewish tradition holds the prophet Samuel to be the author of Judges, but nothing in the text requires this conclusion. Source-critical analysis of Judges is very similar to that of Joshua, suggesting that several early sources were edited into their final form by a later historian.

The writer of Judges presents the history of these times in such a way as to emphasize a literary and theological cycle that repeats itself throughout the book. The cycle begins when the people sin, usually by committing idolatry, and then judgment follows, usually as an enemy invasion. The people repent of their sin, and God raises a deliverer, or judge, who rallies the tribe to defeat the enemy. A period of peace finally follows. This five-point cycle occurs repeatedly throughout the book.

The chronology of the book of Judges presents a problem: If all the time periods cited are taken sequentially, their total time span is too long to fit between the end of the conquest and the beginning of the monarchy. The best solution is to allow some overlapping of judgeships. One hypothesis is that the major judges were sequential, while the minor judges were contemporary with other judges.

The book of Judges also reveals an increasing disunity among the tribes of Israel. This trend can be seen in the days of Deborah when she calls all the tribes to help fight Jabin, the king of Hazor, and four tribes do not respond. Later, when Gideon was pursuing enemies, he asked the inhabitants of two Israelite cities for help. They answered that they did not want to become involved until they could be sure Gideon had won. Still later, when Jephthah was judge, civil war broke out among the tribes.

The period of the judges disintegrated into a time of turmoil and disunity among the tribes.

The issue of kingship is introduced in the book of Judges. Four times in the last chapters the writer complains, "In those days Israel had no king, so the people did whatever seemed right in their own eyes" (Judges 21:25). Israel had functioned as a theocracy during the time of the judges, and the writer is most likely writing during the period of the monarchy. The writer is apparently in favor of the monarchy as a means to bring order to the nation.

> Problems of Incomplete Conquest Noted (1:1–3:6)
> Rule of the Judges (3:5–16:31)
> Migration of the Tribe of Dan (17:1–18:31)
> The Civil War with the Tribe of Benjamin (19:1–21:25)

RUTH   The short book of Ruth is named after the heroine of the story, a Moabitess who marries into the Israelite community and becomes an ancestor of King David. The opening verse sets the story of Elimelech and Naomi's emigration to Moab in "the days when the judges ruled." The family had fled from Israel to escape a famine and had settled in Moab. Elimelech's two sons married local women, Orpah and Ruth, but eventually Elimelech and his sons all die, leaving the three women widowed and childless. Naomi decides to return to her family in Bethlehem but urges her daughters-in-law to remain in Moab to remarry.

As the three women discuss the return to Judah, Naomi is concerned that her daughters-in-law cannot obtain levirate marriages, since she has no more sons and is past the age of childbearing. Levirate marriages took place when a man married his deceased brother's childless widow and fathered children in his brother's name. As Ruth begs Naomi to let her return to Israel with her, she displays her loyalty both for Naomi and for

Naomi's God. After the women arrive in Bethlehem, Boaz, a relative of Elimelech, becomes the protector of the family and marries Ruth in order to raise up sons for his departed relative. Ruth thereby becomes a link in the lineage of David, the king of Israel.

God's concern for all peoples becomes an important theological theme in the book of Ruth. There is no hint of prejudice against Ruth because of her ethnicity. Rather, as Ruth embraced the faith of Naomi, she was honored for her loyalty, suggesting that faith, not nationality, is the critical concern of God. Actual Israelite lineage was not a prerequisite for sharing in the covenant community.

There is no scholarly consensus on the date of this anonymous book, but many favor the time of David since the genealogy in the book ends with him. One episode in the story involves a sandal and requires explanation on the part of the writer, implying that a considerable interval of time elapsed between the actual events and the writing of the story. Wherever the story fits within the period of the judges, the centuries between the setting of the story and the days of the United Monarchy could have been bridged by earlier written sources and oral tradition.

Some scholars suggest that the purpose of the book of Ruth is to explain the inclusion of a foreigner in David's genealogy. Ruth's presence could have been seen as a problem for David's legitimate claim to the throne. Therefore, the writer of the story recounts the events in defense of David's legitimacy, showing that faith, not lineage, makes a true Israelite.

Other scholars regard Ruth as a late story, a novel written to counter what many consider to be harsh treatment of intermarriage by Ezra and Nehemiah at the close of the Old Testament. It is unlikely, however, that the Hebrew canon would include works so diametrically opposed to each other as Ruth and Ezra-Nehemiah. Other scholars date Ruth late because the

Hebrew Bible places her story among the Writings, which tends to have later works.

> The Return of Naomi and Ruth to Bethlehem (1:1-22)
> Ruth Gleans in the Field of Boaz (2:1-23)
> Ruth Seeks Boaz as Her Kinsman-Redeemer (3:1-18)
> The Marriage of Boaz and Ruth (4:1-22)

1 & 2 SAMUEL   The books of Samuel represent what was originally a single composition in the ancient Hebrew canon. The same is true of the books of Kings and of Chronicles. The translators of the Greek Septuagint were most likely the first to divide both Samuel and Kings into two books each, presenting the resulting four books as a complete history of the kings of Israel.

The title *Samuel* is not entirely appropriate for these books, since their history recounts not only the deeds of Samuel, but of Saul and David as well. The traditional view of the Talmud that identifies Samuel as the author of the books is unlikely. Samuel's death is recorded in 1 Samuel, making it impossible for him to have authored the history of 2 Samuel, which takes place after his death. It is possible that 1 Samuel came primarily from the prophet Samuel by means of a book called *The Record of Samuel the Seer,* mentioned in 1 Chronicles 29:29. This work no longer exists, but it could have served as a sourcebook for the writing of the books of Samuel and Chronicles. It may be, however, that the book mentioned in 1 Chronicles simply became 1 and 2 Samuel.

The fact that the books of Samuel cover the lives of Samuel, Saul, and David makes it unlikely that the books as they exist today were written by a person who was contemporary to all three people. In addition, the author's repeated use of the phrase "to this day" further suggests some chronological distance between the final author and the subjects of his history. It is clear that the author was dependent upon already existing sources. There is no clear consensus concerning the identity of the final author and the sources used to write the books of Samuel, although the writer appears to be in favor of David's kingship and hopes to legitimize David's reign through his books.

The books of Samuel relate the history of Israel as it moved from the rule of judges to the rule of kings. The books detail the events of Samuel's birth and call, the loss and return of the ark of the covenant, the institution of the monarchy and the rise of Saul, the rise of David, and various events during David's reign. In addition to recording history, the author also evaluates the rise of the monarchy theologically and prophetically. At times the assessment of the monarchy is positive, but in other places the author shows the monarchy to be far from ideal. By showing this mixed attitude toward the monarchy, the writer supports it as an institution ordained by God but recognizes that the actions of each king may be less than ideal.

> (1 Samuel)
> The Final Days of the Judges (1–7)
> Saul's Anointing and Reign (8–15)
> David's Anointing and Saul's Demise (16–31)
> (2 Samuel)
> David's Early Reign over Judah (1–4)
> David's Successful Reign over All Israel (5–10)
> Moral and Political Decline in David's Household (11–20)
> Appendix of Other Incidents (21–24)

1 & 2 KINGS The books of 1 and 2 Kings, like the books of 1 and 2 Samuel, were originally written as a single document. The translators of the Greek Septuagint divided both Kings and Samuel into two books each, presenting the resulting four books as a complete history of the kings of Israel. The books of Kings can be divided into three major sections: the reign of Solomon, the years of the Divided Kingdom, and the final years of the kingdom of Judah.

The origin of the books of Kings is difficult to discern, and the author or group of authors cannot be identified definitively. Traditional views often elect Ezra or one of the latter prophets as possible candidates for producing the final edition. The books as a whole were certainly composed sometime after the release of Jehoiachin in Babylon (561 B.C.), the final event they record. Thus, the books of Kings must be dated either during the Babylonian exile or, perhaps, during the later period of restoration. Many scholars point out, however, that much of the narrative seems to be of preexilic origin. The author probably compiled 1 and 2 Kings from earlier documents, utilizing the history of Israel to make his theological and prophetic points.

While the development of the books of Kings has a long history that is difficult to trace, the final composition clearly forms a single literary unit, woven together by a strong prophetic and theological theme. The books review the history of Israel's kings from its high point at the end of David's reign to its darkest hour at the time of the Exile. The clear purpose of the composition was not just to relate history, but to explain why the Exile came about. The readers needed an explanation for the traumatic exile to Babylon. The author uses the narrative of Israel's history to show that the Exile was clearly Israel's fault. The books review how the idolatry and wickedness of Israel forced God to punish the nation. The books confess Israel's past sins and praise God for his justice in dealing with his people. The books of Kings also send a prophetic warning to the people who have survived the Exile, convincing them to avoid the sins of their ancestors and to lead lives pleasing to God. And though 2 Kings ends with Israel in exile, it ends with a note of hope. The writer shows that

God's promise to David of an eternal dynasty remains alive as Jehoiachin, one of David's descendants, is raised to a position of prominence while still in exile.

(1 Kings)
Solomon's Reign (1–11)
The Divided Kingdom (12–22)
(2 Kings)
The Divided Kingdom (1:1–16:20)
The Fall of Samaria (17:1–18:12)
Judah Alone (18:13–24:9)
The Fall of Jerusalem (24:10–25:30)

1 & 2 CHRONICLES   The books of 1 and 2 Chronicles were originally written as a single book. The Septuagint translators later divided it into two separate books and called them "things omitted," indicating that the chronicler's record included facts and events omitted by the books of Samuel and Kings. The Septuagint title is no longer used since it is clear that the books are far more than a list of omissions.

The authorship of the Chronicles has traditionally been attributed to Ezra, though the book itself makes no such claim. Its concern with the Levites and temple worship point to a possible Levitical origin. The exact dating of the Chronicles is difficult. Since the last event mentioned is the return from the Exile, the books were probably written soon afterward as an encouragement to those who had returned to rebuild Israel. Some scholars have pointed to a very late date because the genealogy section includes six generations following the Exile. This could push the date to a time as late as 400 B.C. It is possible, however, that this section of the genealogy was added later to update the record for later readers.

It is widely noted that the Chronicles are closely connected with the books of Ezra and Nehemiah. The book of 2 Chronicles ends with the decree of Cyrus, and Ezra begins with the same event. Ezra-Nehemiah clearly extends the history of the Chronicles, and the books contain many literary, linguistic, historical, and theological similarities. Because of this, many scholars hold to the common authorship and literary unity of these books.

Most scholars recognize that the chronicler probably drew from the books of Samuel and Kings, since the parallel passages are often nearly identical. The chronicler's intent, however, was not simply to write a comprehensive history of Israel. Instead, selecting only the historical material that best met the needs of postexilic Israel, the chronicler's central purpose was to encourage Israel to obey God so that they could enjoy God's favor and blessing. The author also wanted to demonstrate God's faithfulness, showing that God had fulfilled the promise given by Jeremiah to restore Israel to the Promised Land. The books review Israel's history, showing that when the people obey God's will and law, they experience great prosperity and peace. But when they disobey God's law, only disaster and suffering result. The chronicler emphasizes the role of the Davidic dynasty to show God's faithfulness to his promises to David and to give hope to the returned exiles concerning the future. The chronicler's emphasis on temple worship reinforces the call to holiness while reminding the people that God has been faithful to reestablish the temple.

The books of Chronicles cover Israel's entire history, beginning with Adam and ending with Israel's return from the Exile. The books naturally divide into four major sections. The first part is made up of genealogies in which the Davidic dynasty is a dominant feature. The second section briefly mentions Saul and then gives an account and assessment of David's reign. The third part recounts the activities of Solomon including the construction of the temple. The final section gives the history of the

Divided Kingdom, primarily emphasizing the Davidic dynasty in Judah. The reports on godly kings are expansive and the deeds of the evil kings are downplayed. The book of 2 Chronicles closes with the destruction of Jerusalem, but, as a sign of hope, it includes at the very end Cyrus's decree to release the Jews.

(1 Chronicles)
Genealogies of the Tribes of Israel (1–9)
Saul's Reign (10)
David's Reign (11–29)
(2 Chronicles)
Solomon's Reign (1:1–9:31)
Kings of Judah (10:1–36:13)
The Captivity and Release (36:14-23)

EZRA-NEHEMIAH   The books of Ezra and Nehemiah are named for the dominant characters in each book. The books of Ezra and Nehemiah were originally considered a single book until Jerome divided them in the Vulgate and called them 1 and 2 Ezra. Tradition identifies Ezra as the author, though there is no direct claim for Ezra's authorship in the text. Regardless of the final editor's identity, it is likely that chapters 7–9 of Ezra and chapters 8–10 of Nehemiah came from Ezra's own memoirs. Chapters 11–13 of Nehemiah most likely came from Nehemiah's own memoirs, since much of this section is written in the first person singular. Due to stylistic and theological similarities, Ezra-Nehemiah and 1 and 2 Chronicles are widely recognized to be the work of the same writer.

Together the books of Ezra and Nehemiah form a history of Israel from the perspective of the postexilic period. The writer's central purpose is to show that God has fulfilled the promise of Jeremiah that God will restore his people to the Land of Promise. God brings about this restoration by moving members of the exiled community to act (Sheshbazzar, Joshua, Zerubbabel, Haggai, Zechariah, Ezra, and Nehemiah) and by stirring the spirits of reigning kings to support Israel's restoration (Cyrus, Darius, and Artaxerxes). The books of Ezra and Nehemiah, like the books of Kings and the Chronicles, emphasize the importance of purity in the restoration community, thus continuing the clear message that sin was the real cause behind the Exile. Ezra and Nehemiah divide naturally into five sections: (1) the return and work under Zerubbabel, (2) the return and work under Ezra, (3) the return of Nehemiah and the rebuilding of the wall, (4) Ezra's reading of the Law and the people's responses, and (5) a report on the dedication of the wall and Nehemiah's final reforms.

(Ezra)
Rebuilding the Temple under Zerubbabel (1–6)
The Return under Ezra (7–10)
(Nehemiah)
Rebuilding the Walls of Jerusalem (1–7)
Restoring Covenant Purity (8–13)

ESTHER The book of Esther is named for its Jewish heroine whose bravery spares the Jewish race from total genocide. The story is set in the reign of the Persian monarch Xerxes, or Ahasuerus (584–465 B.C.). Since Esther and Mordecai and the actions attributed to them in this book are not mentioned in any extant Persian or Greek inscriptions, some have classified this book as a "historical novella" of the second century B.C., written to encourage the kind of Jewish nationalism that Esther models in her dealings with Ahasuerus. However, the author's familiarity with Persian terms and customs from several centuries earlier is surprising if the story was written during Hellenistic times.

The intriguing plot pits Haman, a powerful Persian official, against the Jewish people. Haman's hatred for the Jews had grown out of a personal clash with Mordecai, Esther's cousin and adoptive parent. When a contest is held by King Ahasuerus to find the most beautiful woman in the empire to be his queen, Esther is chosen to appear before the king. Esther pleases the king and gains his favor by revealing an assassination plot against him. In the meantime, Haman devises a plan to eliminate all the Jews from the empire and gains the king's approval. Esther, who had concealed her Jewish nationality from the Persian officials, chooses to reveal her identity to the king in order to save her people. The king is outraged and hangs Haman from his own gallows. Nevertheless, the king feels he cannot alter the edict Haman had pressed him to make, although he does allow the Jews to defend themselves against attack. Only Haman's followers, not the entire Persian army, attack the Jews, and the Jews win a stunning victory.

The outcome of the Jewish victory over Haman was the establishment of the Jewish feast of *Purim*. The name *Purim* comes from Haman's casting of the *pur,* or lot, to determine the day to carry out the plan of destroying the Jews.

Esther is the only book in the Bible not to explicitly mention the name of God. Consequently, some have understood the book to be merely secular history, holding no particular theological significance. Many Jews did not consider Esther to be canonical, as evidenced by the book's absence from the Dead Sea Scrolls. Upon closer examination, however, the outcome of the story does hold theological significance, even if the characters within the book are motivated by nationalism rather than divine compulsion. If Haman's plot had succeeded and the Jewish race had been eliminated, God's redemptive purposes for the nation of Israel would have been thwarted, and the covenant promises would have come to an end.

The Plot to Destroy the Jewish Nation (1–3)
The Plot Exposed (4–7)
The Plot Frustrated (8–10)

. . . . .POETRY AND WISDOM

The books of Poetry and Wisdom, comprised of Job, Psalms, Proverbs, Ecclesiastes, and Song of Songs, were originally included among the Writings in the Hebrew canon. Much of the Writings section was written late in Israel's history, probably sometime after the Babylonian exile. The contents of Psalms and Proverbs, however, clearly represent much earlier writings. A large portion of Psalms and Proverbs was composed during the reigns of David and Solomon, although it is likely that the final collections of these works were compiled much later.

Poetry

A full one-third of the entire Old Testament is written in Hebrew poetic form. Poetry is not limited to the five books listed under Poetry and Wisdom. It is present in most of the Old Testament books, especially among the Prophets. Classical Hebrew poetry, however, usually is not easy to recognize for the average English reader. In the Hebrew text, poetic lines are strung together just like lines of prose, although most English translations helpfully set poetry off from the rest of the text. The following devices characterize classical Hebrew poetry and make it fairly recognizable to Hebrew readers.

Parallelism is the most dominant feature of Hebrew poetry. Parallelism refers to two or more statements that are written to correspond or run parallel to each other. The first statement is generally reinforced or elaborated upon by the second, although various forms of parallelism exist. In synonymous parallelism, the second statement repeats the first using different words. In synthetic parallelism, the second line amplifies or complements the first, but the connection between the two lines is less direct than in the synonymous form. In antithetic parallelism, the second line expresses a contrast to the first in order to reinforce a point. There are other minor forms of parallelism as well.

The nature of *meter* in Hebrew poetry has been a topic of extensive discussion. Scholars agree that meter, as Western culture understands it, does not exist in classical Hebrew poetry. There are no consistent, measured sequences between accented syllables. Hebrew poetry is, however, accentual in regard to meter. In other words, the lines in a poetic sequence contain a consistent number of accented syllables, although the number of unaccented syllables can vary.

With the exception of rhyme and a regular quantitative meter, Hebrew poetry makes use of all the common literary devices of English poetry. *Metaphor, alliteration, onomatopoeia, hyperbole,* and *personification,* to name a few, are commonly found in Hebrew poetry. Hebrew poets often employed the acrostic to aid listeners in memorizing their lyrics. *Chiastic construction,* a series of statements followed by an inverted order of parallel statements, is also common. Since Hebrew poetry is not governed by rhyme and quantitative meter, which changes from language to language, it is especially conducive to translation. The powerful effect of parallelism is not as readily lost in translation as it is with phonic rhyme.

THE PSALMS   The book of Psalms is a diverse collection of one hundred and fifty religious songs used for both private and public worship in ancient Israel. Many are very personal, articulating the writer's sheer joy to be in the sanctuary (84), the frustration of life's inequities (73), the wonderment of nature (19), the anguish caused by grievous sins (51), and numerous other emotions from living day to day. Yet many psalms were also composed for use in public worship, expressing humiliation from Israel's defeat (60), celebration of victory (124), gratitude for God's gracious acts in history (136), and other corporate responses. The emotional tone of the book vacillates between praise and lament, which makes the Psalms an invaluable source for spiritual catharsis.

King David's association with the book of Psalms has been minimized by many scholars due to the assumed late date of the material. While many of the psalms clearly deal with matters that arose long after David's time, David's reputed musical ability and the discovery of some literature from the United Kingdom that closely parallels some of the psalms lend support to David's affiliation. Seventy-three of the psalms are traditionally associated with him.

The book of Psalms is comprised of several smaller collections of songs that were joined into a single book over a long period of time. Some of these collections are still identifiable, including psalms of Korah (42–49), of Asaph (73–83), of David (3–41; 138–145), of ascents (120–134), and the *hallelujah* psalms (111–118; 146–50). The minor collections were eventually incorporated into a larger hymnbook, and the final edition of the book of Psalms appeared after the Exile. The collection was later broken down into five divisions: Book One (1–41), Book Two (42–72), Book Three (73–89), Book Four (90–106), and Book Five (107–150). Each of the first four books concludes with a brief doxology.

The older method of classifying the various psalms was by content, and the categories included messianic, wisdom, imprecatory, royal, and historical psalms. With the development of form criticism, however, scholars have reclassified the psalms by literary types, including community laments, private laments, hymns, entrance liturgies, royal psalms, thank-offering songs, and so forth.

Book One: Songs of Deliverance (1–41)
Book Two: Divine Judgments (42–72)
Book Three: National Hymns of Judah (73–89)
Book Four: The Overruling Kingdom (90–106)
Book Five: Anthems of Praise and Thanksgiving (107–150)

SONG OF SONGS   This intriguing book is a love song or possibly a collection of love songs. Ancient Egyptian literature contains many such collections of songs. The amorous tone of the book is obvious, but the story line is not so easy to follow. The difficulty of reconstructing the story and a few other literary complications have led to three main theories of plot structure: (1) Two lovers, Solomon and the maiden, are courting each other throughout the narrative; (2) Solomon courts the maiden throughout the story, but the maiden remains faithful to her shepherd-lover; and (3) two lovers are courting each other, but no true story line exists.

The purpose of this book has been the center of much heated debate. Many see the Song as celebrating the power of love, for "love is as strong as death" (8:6). Others who believe that the maiden remains faithful to her shepherd-lover interpret the Song more as a celebration of fidelity than of love. Then there are still others who feel that the Song is merely rejoicing in human love, especially sexual love. While it is hard to determine which of the above is the actual intent of the Song, it is doubtful that the Song of Songs was canonized for its celebration of sexual love. More likely, the Song was canonized only after it came to be viewed as an allegory for God's love for Israel.

Bride Describes Herself and Feelings for Her Lover
  (1:1–2:7)
King Invites Bride on a Trip; She Dreams of Losing Him
  (2:8–3:5)

Solomon Describes His Bride (3:6–5:1)
Bride Describes Her Husband (5:2–6:3)
King Describes His Wife (6:4–7:9)
Desires of the Woman (7:10–8:4)
Power of Love (8:5-14)

Wisdom

Wisdom literature has also made its way into the Hebrew canon through the books of Job, Proverbs, and Ecclesiastes. Wisdom literature was common throughout the ancient Near East in two broad types: proverbial wisdom, which is well represented by the Proverbs, and speculative wisdom, which can be found in both Job and Ecclesiastes. Proverbial wisdom is made up of short, pithy sayings, or proverbs, in the form of two-part sentences that give instructions for successful living. Speculative wisdom often employs proverbs, as well as monologues (Ecclesiastes) and dialogues (Job). In such literature, ancient sages contemplate the complexities and ambiguities of human existence and the nature of the relationship between God and man. The questions raised by the sages, however, are always dealt with fairly concretely, remaining within the context of human experience.

PROVERBS   The book of Proverbs forms an instruction manual for successful living in ancient Israel. This collection of wise sayings resembles books that were popular in Egypt for giving advice to the young. The purpose of the book, which is given in the first chapter, is to orient the readers to wise and right ways of living. The underlying principle follows: "Fear of the Lord is the beginning of knowledge" (1:7). The compiler of Proverbs appeals to wisdom as a means of producing a stable and God-fearing society. Most of the Old Testament books address predominantly corporate issues. The book of Proverbs, on the other hand, brings spirituality down to the everyday occurences of life.

The association of Solomon with Proverbs is mentioned several times throughout the book. Although some scholars prefer to dissociate Solomon from the Proverbs, Solomon's era was a time when the proverb was popular in Egyptian and Mesopotamian literature. Solomon, as an educated man, would certainly have been aware of this literature and could have collected and composed his own book of pithy sayings.

Three primary collections comprise the book of Proverbs. The first two sections contain Solomon's proverbs, with the second being compiled by Hezekiah's scribes. The third section of non-Solomonic material was then added later to complete the collection.

> The Voice of Wisdom (1:1–9:18)
> Miscellaneous Proverbs of Solomon (10:1–22:16)
> Words of the Wise (22:17–24:34)
> Second Solomonic Collection (25:1–29:27)
> Words of Agur (30:1-33)
> Words of Lemuel (31:1-31)

JOB   The book of Job poetically considers the problem of innocent suffering and God's sovereignty, making it one of finest literary works in the Bible. The book's author and date of composition are unstated and unknown, since there are no direct references to any historical events that could narrow the range of possibilities. Early Jewish and Christian literature considered Job to be a product of the patriarchal period, based upon such details as Job's wealth being measured in terms of livestock, Job's function as family priest, Job's longevity of life, and Job's mention of the Flood and silence regarding other historical events. But these and other characteristics of the story only point to the antiquity of the story itself, however, and not to the date of its compilation.

A second possibility for the date of Job's composition is that an editor of the exilic or postexilic era adapted a story set in the patriarchal period. It has been argued that some of the language and concepts of the book of Job resemble postexilic thought more than patriarchal thinking. This late date is hard to defend, however, in light of the reference to Job in Ezekiel 14:14.

A third alternative to the above solutions is to concede ignorance as to the date of the story, since the Edomite setting of the story could have preserved for quite some time the cultural and religious distinctives of the patriarchal period. A long-standing pastoral environment would make the date of Job's composition extremely difficult to estimate.

The uncertainties of Job's authorship detract little from the significance of the book. Instead, this only serves to underscore the universal nature of the story. The age-old dilemma of innocent suffering and God's sovereignty has been faced by humankind everywhere throughout time. The author of Job rejects the common Hebrew concept that suffering always stems from sinfulness, and so he portrays Job as a blameless man, whose devotion to God is equally matched by his concern for justice.

Despite Job's innocence, tragedy besets him, and he is forced to consider the reasons for his suffering. Job's four friends then expound the theology of the day regarding human suffering. They, with the possible exception of Elihu, consider all suffering to be the direct result of personal sinfulness, and they urge Job to confess his sins and be freed from his pain. But Job cannot agree with their blanket assumptions. He insists that he is innocent and even questions God's justice until he is soundly rebuked by God himself. In the end, God rebukes the friends for wrongly accusing Job of sinning, and he restores Job's fortunes, giving him twice as many possessions as before.

While several questions are considered throughout the story, such as the justice of God and whether there are any who follow God for who he is rather than for what he gives, the primary question of Job considers why he is suffering when he is completely innocent. All the characters involved in the dialogues are ignorant of the wager made between Satan and God at the beginning of the story, though the reader is made privy to this information. Through the misunderstandings of the three friends and Job, the reader is made aware of his or her own inadequacy to understand the problem of innocent suffering and is encouraged simply to bow humbly before the infinite Creator, recognizing God's omniscience. Job does recognize, however, that while his indictments against God were unwarranted and arrogant, through them he had engendered an intimacy with God that he had not known before.

The book of Job consists of three basic sections: the prologue, which reveals the cosmic setting; the dialogue, which presents the conversation between Job and his friends and God's speech; and the epilogue, which records Job's restoration. The prologue and epilogue are written in prose, while the vast majority of the book, the dialogue, appears in poetic form. No single genre can adequately characterize this fascinating book. It has elements of theodicy, tragedy, parable, comedy, and epic, to name a few.

Prologue (1–2)
Dialogue (3–27)
Three Monologues (28–37)
God's Speeches (38:1–42:6)
Epilogue (42:7-17)

ECCLESIASTES   The book of Ecclesiastes documents "the Teacher's" search for the meaning of life. It is hard to say exactly who "the Teacher" is, although he identifies himself as the son of David, probably implying that he is Solomon. It is difficult to be certain, however, if the writer intends for his readers to really believe that he is Solomon or if he is merely personifying his message through Solomon. It is unlikely that the actual author is King Solomon himself, since he seems unable to change the social abuses he encounters in his lifetime and since the text uses the Persian words for "park" and "decree." The bulk of the text was most likely written sometime after the Babylonian exile, although the frequently repeated saying "Everything is meaningless" may have come from Solomon himself.

As "the Teacher" searches for the meaning of life, he examines life from various angles, trying to discover the source of true satisfaction. The dominant tone of the book is fairly negative, as evidenced by the author's constant reminder that death inevitably overtakes everyone and everything will be done in vain. The author decides from personal experience that all earthly activities, when pursued as ends unto themselves, lead to emptiness and despair. The author also despairs over the inequity of life in which the innocent suffer and the wicked prosper. Part of the author's solution to this dilemma is to avoid extremes in life, not becoming too upset or concerned over the things of this life but, instead, taking all things in moderation. In the end the author virtually surrenders his contemplation and instructs the reader: "Fear God and obey his commands; for this is the duty of every person. God will judge us for everything we do, including every secret thing, whether good or bad" (12:13-14).

Prologue (1:1-11)
The Teacher's Experience (1:12–2:26)
The Teacher's Observation (3:1–4:8)
The Teacher's Counsel (4:9–7:10)
The Teacher's Commendation of Wisdom (7:11–9:18)
Life's Closing Scenes (10:1–12:7)
Epilogue (12:8-12)

⸰ . . . . .THE PROPHETS

The prophets were men and women who functioned as God's messengers to humankind. As a rule, they were laypeople who felt compelled to speak out on religious and social issues of their day. The prophets often castigated the people of Israel for abandoning the covenant God made with them at Sinai. Faithfulness to God and ethical actions toward people were the primary covenant concerns of most of the prophets. They abhorred the idolatry and oppression that had come to characterize Israel by the time of the Late Divided Kingdom. The prophets detested the corruption that permeated the monarchy and the priesthood and railed against these abuses.

The prophets generally employed both foretelling and "forthtelling" in their messages. Foretelling refers to predictions given by the prophet from God concerning future events that were often tragic in nature. Foretelling was used both to verify the prophet's validity and to generate repentance on the part of the listeners. Forth-telling, on the other hand, involved stating what the nation was doing wrong and what God required from the people to correct the situation. Forth-telling usually formed the bulk of a prophet's message.

There were many prophets throughout Israel's history, such as Samuel, Elijah, and Elisha, and some of them have had their oracles collected into the books that bear their names. Most of the prophets' oracles have been written in poetic form, making them easier for people to remember.

Early Prophets (Late Divided Kingdom)

AMOS   The book of the prophet Amos contains oracles against the nations surrounding Israel, oracles against Israel itself, and five symbolic visions. Other oracles are fitted around these clusters. The oracles against the nations follow a standard form of arraignment, judgment, and punishment pronounced. The first four visions of Amos also follow a common structure, with visions one and two being paired as well as visions three and four.

Amos came from a village in Judah, where he was a shepherd and tender of sycamore trees. During the reign of Jeroboam II of Israel, Amos prophesied from the notorious sanctuary at Bethel, indicting the neighbors of Israel, the oppressors of the poor, and Jeroboam II himself. Amos's indictments angered Amaziah, the priest at Bethel, who accused Amos of plotting against Jeroboam.

The reign of Jeroboam II, while very prosperous politically and economically, was fraught with social injustice, sexual impropriety, and empty religiosity. Amos railed against these sins and called the people of Israel to repentance. If Israel did not repent, Amos warned of a coming "day of the Lord" in which the nation would be overtaken and the people would be exiled to a foreign land. God would match this destruction, however, by restoring the nation once again.

> Oracles against the Nations (1:3–2:16)
> Oracles against Israel (3:1–6:14)
> Three Visions (7:1-9)
> Encounter with Amaziah (7:10-17)
> Fourth Vision (8:1-3)
> Four Oracles (8:4-14)
> Fifth Vision (9:1)
> Theology of Creation and Redemption (9:2-15)

HOSEA The book of the prophet Hosea condemns Israel through a symbolic biography of the prophet himself. The book poetically recounts Hosea's marriage to a prostitute and the birth of his three children. Hosea's wife then regresses to her unfaithful pattern of life, and Hosea redeems her from her resulting poverty and deplorable lifestyle. The second half of the book elaborates on this theme, comparing Israel to a prostitute and indicting the nation for its many sins.

Hosea also prophesied during the reigns of Jeroboam II in Israel and of Uzziah, Jotham, Ahaz, and Hezekiah of Judah. He was a contemporary of Amos, Isaiah, and Micah. Not much is known of Hosea other than his marital experiences, but it is generally assumed that he was from Israel, given his extensive knowledge of the Northern Kingdom. He most likely prophesied from one of the popular sanctuaries at Bethel, Dan, Gilgal, or Samaria. Hosea's condemnation of idolatry did not please his listeners, and he was quickly labeled a fool and a madman.

Many have taken Hosea's marriage to be a parable or a vision, yet the book itself presents the story as an actual event. Given the eccentric nature of many prophets, it would not be too difficult to imagine the story as actual history. In either case, the message of the book is clear: God loves Israel in spite of the nation's idolatrous affairs and unfaithfulness, and he desires that Israel repent and return to following him. The story symbolizes how God has chosen Israel as his lover, and the children that have come from their marriage represent the stages of Israel's removal from God. Israel is unfaithful to her lover by worshiping Baal and giving *him* what rightfully belongs to God. God will reveal Israel's sin, but he also desires to redeem the nation from its shameful practices and to restore Israel to himself.

> Hosea's Marriage and the Birth of His Children (1:1-9)
> Israel Is Judged and the Covenant Is Renewed (1:10–2:23)
> Reunion of Hosea and His Adulterous Wife (3:1-5)
> Hosea's Message to Israel (4:1–14:9)

JONAH The book of Jonah is strikingly different from the rest of the early prophets in that it is a story about the prophet himself, rather than a collection of prophetic utterances. The only semblance of a prophetic oracle throughout the narrative is "Forty days from now Nineveh will be destroyed!" (3:4). The story follows Jonah from the moment of his prophetic call from God, to his attempt to evade his calling, to his ministry in Nineveh and finally to his dialogue with God outside the city.

Very little is known about Jonah's personal life except for what is given in the book of Jonah. Both Jonah 1:1 and 2 Kings 14:25 identify his father as Amittai, and 2 Kings 14:25 identifies his hometown as Gath-hepher, near Nazareth of Galilee. Jonah prophesied during the reign of Jeroboam II of Israel when Assyria was experiencing a period of weakness. The date of the book's composition is disputed, but its reference to Nineveh in the past tense may indicate that it was written sometime after Nineveh's fall in 612 B.C.

The book of Jonah has been variously interpreted as allegory, as history, and as parable. As allegory, Jonah could represent Israel, and each event in the story would correspond to some facet of Israel's history. The primary message of the story would be the failure of Israel to act as the true chosen people among the nations. As both history and parable, the message is essentially that Israel should not be hesitant to share with other nations their belief in the God of Israel, for God's grace will not be withheld from anyone who is truly repentant.

Jonah's First Calling to Be a Prophet (1:1-17)
Jonah's Prayer and Deliverance from the Great Fish
    (2:1-10)
Jonah's Second Calling to Be a Prophet (3:1-9)
Jonah's Response to Nineveh's Deliverance (3:10–4:5)
Jonah's Prayer and God's Response (4:1-5)
Final Dialogue between God and Jonah (4:6-11)

Later Prophets (Judah Alone)

ISAIAH   The book of Isaiah is an anthology of the prophet's oracles collected over the years of his long ministry. The book is arranged in two volumes (chapters 1–33 and 34–66) that are organized to mirror each other in content. The first volume is divided into four units. Unit One details the spiritual condition of Israel and Judah, which is characterized by idolatry and social oppression that is made even more detestable by empty religiosity. Unit Two condemns Israel's enemies and foretells their destruction. Isaiah was deeply moved for these nations, however, as he contemplated the judgments of God upon them. Unit Three continues to address the surrounding nations, but it gives them hope that God will include them in salvation. Unit Four addresses Jerusalem, warning the citizens against turning to Egypt for help against the Assyrians, and concludes with a sketch of the new era in which God would be king.

The second volume contains units Five, Six, and Seven. Unit Five describes the age to come, in which Israel would become the nation that truly follows God, and the surrounding nations would come to know God through Israel. Unit Six forms a historical appendix that describes Assyria's unsuccessful campaign against Jerusalem, Hezekiah's illness and recovery, and the Babylonian envoys' visit to Hezekiah upon his recovery. Unit Six concludes with a prophecy that Judah will go into Babylonian exile, thus bridging the material to the next unit. Unit Seven brings the book of Isaiah to a close with three short subdivisions of material. The first section announces Judah's release from captivity and the manner in which God will bring this about. The second section of this unit uses three servant songs to describe Judah's true deliverer, a suffering servant. The third and final section imagines a restored Jerusalem and an age when God will extend salvation to the whole world.

Isaiah's prophetic career began in the year of Uzziah's death (740 B.C.). At this time Israel and Judah had reached a turning point. A glorious era of prosperity and national security had concluded, and clouds of doom were gathering in the direction of the expanding empire of Assyria. The era of military success and national strength made it difficult to convince Israel and Judah that their political fortunes were determined not by weapons or well-trained troops, but by faithfulness to God. Nevertheless, Isaiah preached this unpopular message.

The authorship of the book of Isaiah has been argued intensely among scholars. Many scholars believe that chapters 1–39, for the most part, were written or spoken by the historical Isaiah, and chapters 40–66 by an anonymous prophet of the Exile. Various factors have led to this belief, including very different emphases between the two sections and the specific naming of individuals in predictive prophecy passages. Other scholars, however, still hold the view that the historical Isaiah contributed to both sections of the book. The mirror image of the two volumes mentioned above gives strong support for single authorship.

Oracles of Judgment and Hope (1:1–12:6)
Oracles against the Nations (13:1–23:18)
Eschatological Judgments and Triumphs (24:1–27:13)
Oracles of Judgment against Jerusalem and Egypt
(28:1–33:24)
Eschatological Judgment and Blessing (34:1–35:10)
Historical Bridge (36:1–39:8)
Oracles of Consolation (40:1–66:24)

MICAH The book of the prophet Micah falls neatly into three major sections, each beginning with the imperative "hear." Each division opens with an oracle of doom and closes with an oracle of hope. Throughout the book, Micah condemns false prophets, evil leaders, and complacent priests. Apparently Micah or his followers were also in contact with Isaiah or his followers, since both books contain a few identical verses.

Micah, a contemporary of Isaiah, prophesied during the reigns of Jotham, Ahaz, and Hezekiah. He came from the small town of Moresheth-gath. Micah was outraged at the corruption and lethargy of the leaders and priests and summoned them to appear before the court of God to plead their case. Micah's message was not a call to repentance, but a pronouncement of judgment upon Judah. God desires obedience rather than sacrifice, and so the nation must be shaken out of its religious slumber. The bloated self-confidence of the leaders and priests would be shattered by exile to Babylon, and the false prophets would no longer receive visions.

Exile and Restoration (1:1–2:13)
Judah's Fall and Restoration (3:1–5:15)
Concluding Indictment, Lament, and Promise (6:1–7:20)

ZEPHANIAH The book of Zephaniah is comprised of two major sections. The first section is a collection of oracles against Judah and the surrounding nations. It opens and closes with a prophecy that God's judgment will be universal, not merely confined to Judah. Like Amos, Zephaniah warns of the impending "day of the Lord," when Judah would be judged for its wicked deeds. The second section contains promises of salvation for Judah and the nations. Like many of the prophets, Zephaniah interweaves his oracles of judgment with his promises of salvation.

At the beginning of the book, Zephaniah traces his ancestry back four generations to King Hezekiah. The prophet conducted his ministry during the reign of Josiah, king of Judah. Evidence in the book suggests that it was composed before Josiah's reform

of 621 B.C., since the religious synthesis between the faith of
God and the cult of Baal characterized the times. Zephaniah
speaks about disaster that will befall Judah, but he never names
the enemy that will bring it about.

Zephaniah's "day of the Lord" was a day of reckoning for
Judah's pagan religious practices and social injustices. Yet the
prophet held out a thread of hope to Judah as well. If the people
of Judah truly repent, perhaps God would be merciful to them
and their judgment would be repealed.

Universal Judgment (1:1–3:8)
Promises of Salvation (3:9-20)

JEREMIAH   Jeremiah's oracles are arranged according to
thematic rather than chronological criteria. What is now called
the book of Jeremiah is actually a collection of three books, two
biographical sections, and a historical appendix. Book One contains the basic collection of oracles, which details the sins of
Judah and describes the forces that will come from the north to
execute judgment upon the nation. The name of the foe is identified at the end of the section as Babylon. Jeremiah's personal
"confessions" are distributed throughout this first book, expressing deep emotional frustration over the prophet's ministry. A biographical interlude follows, containing stories about Jeremiah's
trial for treason, his conflict with Hananiah the prophet, and his
letter to the exiles in Babylon.

Book Two, called the "Book of Consolation," is composed
mostly in poetry and describes the restoration of Judah. The second biographical interlude follows the second book, detailing
events surrounding the siege and fall of Jerusalem. Book Three
contains Jeremiah's oracles against the nations and a defense of
his reputation as prophet to the nations. Finally, a historical
appendix concludes the book with more details about the Babylo-

nian siege of Jerusalem, the number of captives deported to Babylonia, and the release of Jehoiachin from prison in Babylon.

Jeremiah's long career as a prophet extended through the reigns of the last five kings of Judah. He was in constant dialogue with these kings, expressing approval for Josiah's reforms, enraging Jehoiakim with doomsday forecasts, and being incarcerated by Zedekiah for spreading discontent.

Jeremiah witnessed the fall of Jerusalem and consoled the survivors. Jeremiah had a gift for vivid symbolic gesture, such as carrying a yoke to symbolize the nation's impending exile.

While Jeremiah preached a message of judgment and destruction for Jerusalem's idolatry, his message was not merely one of doom. He preached a strong message of hope as well. Jeremiah promised that after a period of seventy years, God would allow the exiles to return home, and a new covenant would be established with them. This new covenant would be written on tablets of flesh rather than on tablets of stone. Obedience would then come from the heart.

> Book One: The Basic Collection of Prophecies (1:1–25:38)
> First Biographical Interlude (26:1–29:32)
> Book Two: The Book of Consolation (30:1–31:30)
> Second Biographical Interlude (32:1–45:5)
> Book Three: The Oracles against the Nations (46:1–51:64)
> Historical Appendix (52:1-34)

NAHUM Nahum's oracles celebrate the capture of the Assyrian capital by the Babylonians. The fall of Nineveh became a sign to Nahum that God was indeed just and that he would punish those who persecute the innocent. The subject matter and literary structure of Nahum are mutually dependent upon each other. The book opens with a contrast between God as Avenger and God as Savior. The book then moves on to show how these two roles are perfectly illustrated through Nineveh's fall, revealing God's vengeance for Assyrian atrocities and God's salvation for the nation of Judah. Nahum constructs a graphic word picture of the demise of Nineveh and a moving lament over the fallen city. The prophet mourns for both nations.

Little personal information is given about the prophet Nahum, except that he is from the city of Elkosh, whose location is uncertain. The book itself, however, can be dated with a fair degree of accuracy, since it vividly describes an actual historical event. The book was most likely written near the fall of Nineveh in 612 B.C.

> Character Description of God (1:1-8)
> Address to Nineveh's Leaders (1:9-11)
> Address to Judah (1:12-13)
> Address to Nineveh (1:14)
> Address to Judah (1:15)
> Address to Nineveh (2:1–3:19)

HABAKKUK   The book of Habakkuk portrays the prophet as questioning God for the rise of the Chaldeans, who were almost as evil as the Assyrians before them. Why would God use such an evil empire to punish the nation of Judah? The two major divisions of the book are introduced as the oracles of the prophet Habakkuk, and then the oracles alternate between the prophet's prayers and God's answers, with occasional interruptions by words of condemnation or admonition from Habakkuk. The first division contains two such cycles, and the second division concludes the book with one more cycle of prayer and response. In the end, God assures Habakkuk that justice will be meted out in time, and so the righteous must simply continue living by faith in God.

Little information is known of the prophet Habakkuk. He is

identified as a prophet in the first verse of his book. Since such direct identification of a prophet is rarely made in the Hebrew Bible, some interpreters take it as an indication that Habakkuk was one of the professional prophets who made their living by prophesying at the temple or royal court.

First Prayer and Answer (1:1-11)
Second Prayer and Answer (1:12–2:5)
Five Woes against the Chaldeans (2:6-20)
Third Prayer and Answer (3:1-15)
Prophet's Word of Confidence (3:16-19)

LAMENTATIONS The book of Lamentations is perhaps the most refined literature of all the prophetic books. Originally included among the Writings rather than the Prophets, the entire book is a lament over the fall of Jerusalem and over the horrific suffering that followed in its wake. The book is comprised of five poems of twenty-two verses each. The first four poems form Hebrew acrostics, using each letter of the Hebrew alphabet to begin a new verse. The poems' graphic imagery forces the reader to imagine the ghastly atrocities that occurred in the city.

Unlike all the other prophetic books, Lamentations does not name its author. Tradition has ascribed the book to Jeremiah, and many features of the lament resemble the prophet's own book. It is difficult to be certain, however, who compiled the poems into their final form. It is generally assumed that the book was compiled sometime within a generation after the fall of Jerusalem.

While the book of Lamentations is not prophecy in the sense of a warning and a call to repentance, it is prophetic in the way that it places blame for the event upon the false prophets and priests of Jerusalem. Like Jeremiah, the author of Lamentations condemns all the religious leaders who closed their eyes to the idolatry and immorality that characterized the nation. The fall of Jerusalem merely signified that God had tolerated Judah's wickedness long enough, and now judgment had come.

Jerusalem after the Fall (1)
God's Anger (2)
Judah's Lament (3)
Jerusalem's Ruin (4)
Final Lament (5)

OBADIAH   The single oracle of Obadiah condemns the neighboring nation of Edom, probably for its ruthless pillage of Jerusalem after the city had fallen to the Babylonians. The book opens with the announcement that God has sent a messenger among the nations summoning them to battle against Edom. The rest of the book contains a message that God directs to Edom.

Nothing else is known about the prophet himself, but his single oracle is charged with powerful emotions stemming from the sibling rivalry between Jacob and Esau. Jacob is Israel's patriarch, and Edom had descended from Esau. The two nations had a long history of antagonism, and Edom was often listed among the nations that the prophets condemned. Obadiah rails against them as well, pronouncing that justice would someday be served, and the Edomites would be repaid in kind for their deeds.

Indictment of Edom for Pride (1-4)
Announcement of Edom's "day of the Lord" (5-9)
Description of Judah's "day of the Lord" (10-14)
A Second Announcement of Edom's "day of the Lord"
    (15-18)
Promise of Judah's Repatriation (19-21)

Postexilic Prophets

EZEKIEL Similar to the books of Isaiah and Jeremiah, the book of the prophet Ezekiel may consist of two volumes. Three clear divisions are evident, with the first division comprising the first volume and the second and third divisions making up the second volume. The first division recounts the prophet's call and the fall of Jerusalem; the second contains oracles against the surrounding nations; and the third section envisions the restoration of Israel.

Known as the prophet of the Exile, Ezekiel was a man of priestly heritage who was taken to Babylonia in 597 B.C., along with King Jehoiachin and ten thousand other exiles. Five years into the Exile, Ezekiel received a call to be a prophet to the exiled community. Some of his oracles are meticulously dated to the very day of their composition, making this book one of most precisely dated in the prophetic corpus.

Ezekiel's task was to offer encouragement to the Jews in Babylon during the dark days of the Exile. While Ezekiel's book contains many passages regarding sin and judgment, the book is overwhelmingly positive, looking beyond the present national crisis to the future when God would restore the land and its people. Ezekiel uses allegory, parables, and symbolic actions to communicate the reasons for the nation's present suffering and to assure the people of a future hope. Ezekiel offers a penitential prayer for the nation in order to prepare them for the future when God would again inhabit a new temple at Jerusalem.

Judgment on Israel (1–24)
Judgment on the Nations (25–32)
Restoration of Israel (33–48)

DANIEL The book of Daniel was also placed among the Writings in the Hebrew canon, although it was considered prophecy. The book easily divides into two equal parts. The first section chronologically relates various incidents experienced by Daniel and his friends while in exile in Babylon. This section is dominated by historical narrative and reflects the cultural contexts in which the events occur. The second section describes four apocalyptic visions that Daniel saw in his later years. The apocalyptic imagery in these chapters uses symbols and numbers to represent significant events.

The book's structure can also be defined by the use of Hebrew, the native language of Israel, and Aramaic, the international language of the times. The book opens in Hebrew, shifts to Aramaic in the middle section, and returns again to Hebrew in conclusion. The Aramaic center of the book overlaps both the historical and the revelational sections of the book, suggesting the book's literary unity. This shift between Hebrew and Aramaic is reflective of the contents of each section. The Hebrew sections deal with topics more directly related to Israel while the Aramaic section relates information concerning the great empires and the eventual culmination of world history.

The book of Daniel has been dated anywhere from the time of the Exile to the second century B.C. Daniel's actual authorship is obviously dependent upon which date a scholar prefers. According to the book, Daniel served as adviser to the rulers of Babylonia and Persia. While many accuse the book of various historical discrepancies, most of these problems have been satisfactorily resolved by archaeology. The evidence is not conclusive to eliminate the possibility that Daniel himself contributed to the book bearing his name.

The message of the book of Daniel assumes what has been called an *apocalyptic* world view. This view, which can be found in later Jewish writings as well, presupposes that God, who created the world and sustains it, controls the events of history and will bring them to an appointed end, judging the wicked and rewarding the righteous. Daniel shows the Jews, as well as a series of heathen kings, that God is in control of history. The rise and fall of powerful leaders and nations takes place under God's controlling hand, and history will come to its final culmination in God's timing. While the righteous may suffer periods of oppression and discouragement, the time is coming when they will be vindicated.

Historical Section: Daniel and His Friends (1–6)
Prophetic Section: Daniel's Visions and Prayer (7–12)

HAGGAI   Through elevated prose, the book of the prophet Haggai calls the people of Israel to rebuild the temple. Structurally, the book is composed of four messages, each introduced by the date of the oracle and the phrase "the Lord sent this message through the prophet Haggai." The first message describes the agricultural failure that plagued the community; the second message compares the glory of a new temple with the glory of the old temple; the third message draws some lessons from ritual law; and the fourth message promises that God will bring about his will by a powerful shaking of the heavens and the earth.

Since the book gives specific dates for each of the oracles, the date of the book's composition can be determined fairly accurately. It was most likely compiled around 520 B.C., shortly after the return of the exiles from Babylonia. Information about Haggai himself, however, is not as specific. He is called a prophet, along with Zechariah, who prophesied around the same time. Haggai relayed his messages to Zerubbabel, governor of Judah, and to Joshua (Jeshua), the high priest.

In contrast to the attitudes of the preexilic prophets, Haggai's pro-priesthood position is striking. Many prophets railed against the priesthood for its moral corruption and spiritual lethargy, and much of the blame for the Exile fell on the priesthood. The Exile apparently purged the priesthood of its past sins for a while, however, and the prophet Haggai urged the people to support the reinstitution of the priesthood and its duties. Haggai fostered enthusiasm for rebuilding the temple and reinstated the sacrificial system. Soon after Haggai's appeals, the reconstruction effort was underway. The prophet was careful to note, however, that ritual holiness could not transfer moral holiness to the new community. *That* holiness came only by moral obedience.

> Message One: Haggai's Response to a Popular Saying (1:1-15)
> Message Two: Glory of New and Old Temple Is Compared (2:1-9)
> Message Three: Moral Lessons from Ritual Law (2:10-19)
> Message Four: Hope for Revival of the Davidic Dynasty (2:20-33)

ZECHARIAH   The book of the prophet Zechariah affirms that the nation of Israel was exiled for its sinful practices, but also that God himself would someday transform the nation and usher in a new age of holiness upon the whole earth. The book divides into two halves, the first half being composed in prose and the second half including both prose and poetry. The first half of the book contains an introduction, eight night visions, and oracles about fasting. Several of the eight visions focus on the reconstruction of the temple and the reinstitution of the priesthood. The first emphasizes the need for judgment to fall upon the nations who oppose Israel and who hinder the reconstruction efforts. The second half of Zechariah contains oracles regarding the age to come when God will transform Israel into a truly holy society, and the nations will come to worship God in Jerusalem.

The prophet Zechariah, a priest by profession, complemented the prophet Haggai and his efforts to restore the temple. Both are mentioned together in the book of Ezra. According to the dates in the first half of his book, Zechariah prophesied from 520 to 518 B.C. There are no dates, however, for the oracles in the second half of the book, so these could have been written well beyond the reconstruction of the temple in 520 B.C.

Like Ezekiel many years earlier, Zechariah's primary emphasis, while recognizing Israel's past sinfulness, was to encourage the Jews and to assure them of their coming restoration. Zechariah defended and affirmed the preexilic prophets who condemned Israel for its wickedness. He endorsed the belief that the Exile was a result of the nation's sins. Zechariah also prophesied of a new era, however, in which God himself would look after Israel's spiritual state. The reconstruction of the temple would be the dawning of this new era and a royal figure, described in the second half of the book as a "shepherd" to the flock of Israel, would reign over a new kingdom of perfect harmony between God and Israel.

Eight Night Visions (1–6)
Reflections on Fasting (7–8)
Oracles concerning a Humble King (9–11)
Future Judgment and Redemption for Jerusalem and the
     Nations (12–14)

JOEL   The book of the prophet Joel falls into two halves, the first being a lament over a locust plague that has just ravaged Judah, and the second being God's response to the lament. The locust plague immediately becomes a metaphor for an invading army that devours the countryside of Judah. Joel then enlarges the imagery even further by interpreting the plague as a portent of God's approaching judgment. The prophet calls for the people to repent, although the exact nature of their sins is not disclosed. Joel then imagines what God's response will be when the people repent. He paints a vivid portrait of a new day when God will drive out Judah's enemies and restore the land to a very fruitful state, while the nations that oppress Judah remain desolate.

Like several other prophets, Joel left us no personal information about himself aside from the name of his father, Pethuel. Some have suspected that he was a priest, but in the first and second chapters he sets himself apart from them. The most that can be said of Joel is that he was a prophet who, like the postexilic prophets, held the temple and priesthood in high regard. Likewise, the date of Joel's oracles has been the source of much debate. It has been dated anywhere from the ninth to the fourth centuries B.C. The book has affinities with the oracles of Amos, suggesting an early date, yet there is also mention of Edomite hostility and of the Greeks, suggesting a later date.

The book of Joel has been interpreted as a historical event, as an allegorical story, and as apocalyptic prophecy. Regardless of the interpretive framework used, the message remains the same: God is about to punish Judah for some undisclosed sin, but he will bring about a great restoration when the nation repents. A great new day is coming when the people will worship God, who will pour out his Spirit upon all men and women, and Judah's enemies, both natural and human, will be eliminated.

> Lament over the Plague of Locusts (1:1–2:17)
> God's Response to Judah's Repentance (2:18-32)
> Judgment on the Unrepentant Nations (3:1-21)

MALACHI   The book of the prophet Malachi calls both the people and the priesthood of Israel to obey God's commands. Two or three generations had passed since the restoration of the temple and the priesthood, and now enthusiasm for obeying God had waned. The people were falling back into their sinful patterns, and the priesthood was losing its integrity as well. Malachi prophesied against this religious apathy, using six arguments and rebuttals between the people and God. Malachi plays out disputes over love, honor, faithlessness, divine justice, repentance, and service to God. He warns of a future "day of the Lord," when the wicked will be judged and the righteous will be rewarded. The book concludes by making reference to the persons of Moses and Elijah, the exemplars of Law and Prophecy.

Little is known about the prophet Malachi. Some scholars have even suggested that the prophet is merely a figurative character, especially in light of his name, which means "my messenger." All of the other prophetic books, however, are named after actual figures in Israel's history, so it is unlikely that Malachi is merely figurative. The book itself was most likely composed sometime around the reforms of Ezra and Nehemiah (ca. 450 B.C.). It is difficult to ascertain whether the book was compiled before Ezra's arrival, during Ezra's reforms, or during Nehemiah's governorship.

The book of Malachi brings the Hebrew canon to a close with a prophecy concerning the arrival of Elijah, who would come and prepare Israel for the "great and terrible day of the Lord."

> First Disputation: On Love (1:1-5)
> Second Disputation: On Honor (1:6–2:9)
> Third Disputation: On Faithlessness (2:10-16)
> Fourth Disputation: On Divine Justice (2:17–3:5)
> Fifth Disputation: On Repentance (3:6-12)
> Sixth Disputation: On Serving God (3:13–4:3)
> Appendix: Moses and Elijah (4:4-6)

. . . . .LETTERS OF THE NEW TESTAMENT

Most of the New Testament books are not really books at all but first-century letters (epistles). With the exception of the Gospels and Acts and possibly Hebrews and Revelation, all of the New Testament books follow the standard format of the day for personal and official correspondence.

Some of the New Testament letters were written as personal letters, beginning with (1) an identification of the writer and (2) a salutation to the recipient of the letter, followed by (3) a blessing or word of well-wishing to the recipient and perhaps a few details about the time and place of writing. After this introduction, (4) the body of the letter follows. A few (5) greetings to specific individuals usually conclude the letter, along with (6) a final benediction. Archaeologists have uncovered hundreds of Hellenistic letters that follow this general format. Paul's letter to Philemon and the second and third letters of John are the best examples of personal letters in the New Testament.

Some Hellenistic writers used the letter form as a literary vehicle to present certain themes. This form allowed for a personal presentation of a weighty topic without sounding pretentious. Most of the New Testament letters follow this format. They have the same basic form as a personal letter, but their contents are not just personal exchanges—they develop substantial discourses about spiritual truths. Some of Paul's epistles could even be called treatises. Romans is a treatise on God's eternal plan for his chosen people, and Ephesians is a treatise on the great mystery of Christ and the church.

The Letters of Paul to the Churches

The letters of the apostle Paul comprise nearly one-third of the entire New Testament. These epistles are vital to the church because they establish Christian doctrine and explain Christian practice. In the following summaries, Paul's epistles are presented in chronological order in order to help the reader grasp the historical development of Paul's work and writings. The history of this development is intricately linked with the history of Paul's life and travels as presented in the book of Acts. Therefore the reader is encouraged to study each letter in conjunction with the circumstances that surrounded its composition.

GALATIANS   Paul's epistle to "the churches of Galatia" (1:2) has been called the "Magna Carta" of spiritual emancipation. Martin Luther called it "my own epistle." Through the concrete (and potentially explosive) context of real-life events, Paul resolves the dispute over justification by faith. The decision established in this epistle became the touchstone for the rest of Paul's letters.

The actual region of Galatia to which the letter refers is often debated. The official region of Galatia is a district in Asia Minor bordering on Phrygia, Pontus, Bithynia, Cappadocia, and Pamphylia. Most modern scholars consider the area mentioned in the letter to be southern Galatia, which encompassed the cities visited by Paul on his first and second missionary journeys. Other scholars define the area as northern Galatia. Likewise, the date of the letter's composition is disputed. Much of the debate hinges on a meeting at Jerusalem mentioned in Galatians 2:1-10. If this meeting is identical to the Jerusalem Council recorded in Acts 15, then Paul probably wrote this epistle around A.D. 56. If the two meetings are different, then this epistle may well have been written as early as A.D. 49, making it the first of Paul's letters.

The Galatians had received Paul's gospel message with joy at first, but they soon wavered in their allegiance to his teaching when some false teachers instructed them to observe the laws of Moses in order to please God (2:11-13). These false teachers almost convinced the Galatians to undergo circumcision, a key act of obedience to Mosaic law. They also accused Paul of falsely representing himself as a divinely commissioned apostle when, in fact, he was but a messenger sent by the apostles in

Jerusalem. They added that his teaching contradicted that of Peter and James and should not be accepted.

Paul's purpose, then, in writing this epistle was (1) to defend his apostolic authority; (2) to counteract the false teachers' influence in Galatia, showing that their doctrine destroyed the very essence of Christianity; and (3) to strengthen the Galatian believers in their Christian faith. Paul had already confronted the false teachers and the Galatians face-to-face, and now he was writing to finally put an end to the whole debate.

The tone of this epistle combines the two extremes of sternness and tenderness. Paul's beginning is abrupt, reflecting the urgency of his concerns. As he develops his thoughts, however, a warmhearted tenderness can be found in Paul's admonitions. The epistle ends with a final warning against false teaching and a closing benediction.

> Introduction (1:1-10)
> God's Special Revelation to Paul (1:11–2:21)
> Freedom through Grace Rather Than the Law (3:1–4:31)
> Freedom in the Spirit (5:1–6:10)
> Conclusion (6:11-18)

1 THESSALONIANS The first letter of Paul to the Thessalonians urges the believers to lead lives worthy of the kingdom that would soon be established at the return of Christ. Paul addresses this young church as a father would instruct a growing child, commending them for their strengths and admonishing them in their weaknesses.

Paul probably wrote this epistle from Corinth, where Timothy and Silas rejoined him soon after he arrived in A.D. 50. It was written not long after the church was founded at Thessalonica, as indicated by Paul's comment that he was taken from them for a short time (2:17). At the time, Thessalonica was the capital of the

Roman district of Macedonia, and it enjoyed a thriving economy. The Thessalonian church had been established by Paul after his imprisonment and flogging at Philippi. The Thessalonian believers received the gospel joyfully, despite persecution from their own countrymen and from many Jews (1:6; 2:13-16). The church continued to grow, and the gospel spread from there throughout Macedonia, Achaia, and elsewhere (1:7-8). Paul eventually moved on to Athens and then to Corinth, where he wrote this epistle.

Timothy brought a good report to Paul concerning the Thessalonian church. They abounded in faith and love and longed to see Paul, just as Paul longed to see them (3:6-10). Thus they were healthy in the faith, but they also needed Paul's guidance in several matters. Apparently some among them needed to be warned against adultery (4:3-7) and revelry (5:5-8). Some may have lacked respect for their leaders (5:12-13), and others were obstructing the work of the Spirit (5:19-20). Paul corrected these believers while affirming his love for them. Some whose relatives had died needed comfort and instruction concerning whether their relatives would also be included in the kingdom, since they had died before Christ's return.

Throughout the letter Paul remains appropriately calm and equable, since he is only dealing with various practical offenses rather than significant doctrinal controversies. Overall, the letter is very encouraging and affirming of the young church.

Salutation (1:1)
Reputation of the Thessalonian Church (1:2-10)
Review of Paul's Relationship with Them (2:1–3:13)
Addressing Problems within the Church (4:1–5:11)
Conclusion (5:12-28)

2 THESSALONIANS In his second letter to the Thessalonians, Paul encourages those who are being persecuted for the gos-

pel and clarifies his earlier statements regarding the return of
Christ. Apparently, after Paul had first written to the Thessalonians, many believers became confused about the return of Christ
and misunderstood Paul's statements in the first letter. Others
stirred up the church with rumors that Christ had already
returned. Some professed to know by the Spirit (2:2) that this
was so; others alleged that Paul had said this when he was with
them. It seems that there was even a letter falsely ascribed to
Paul that circulated among the believers, stirring up more confusion. Some members of the church were even neglecting their
daily work, possibly in anticipation of Christ's impending return.

Paul corrects these misunderstandings of Christ's return by
asserting that there must first be a time of great rebellion when
"the man of lawlessness" would be revealed. When he is finally
revealed, the Lord will destroy him. Paul then explains how
those who refuse to obey the gospel are being deceived by this
same evil power. It is difficult to know exactly what Paul is writing about, but the overall message is clear—Jesus Christ has not
yet returned, and so believers must continue living their lives in
obedience to the gospel. No one was to become lazy, depending
entirely upon others for their food. Paul also cautions the church
to look for his own signature on any letters ascribed to him, so
that they are not deceived again.

It is almost certain that this second letter to the Thessalonians
was written in Corinth shortly after the first letter (ca. A.D. 51).
The epistle was written jointly with Timothy and Silas, who
were with Paul for only a short while.

The distinguishing mark of this letter is Paul's use of apocalyptic imagery in his discussion about the return of Christ. Paul
draws upon imagery resembling that of Daniel, Zechariah, and
the apocalyptic passages of the Gospels (which were written
later than this letter).

Salutation (1:1-2)

Thanksgiving for Their Faith, Love, and Perseverance
(1:3-12)

Signs of the End Times (2:1-17)

Final Exhortations and Greetings (3:1-18)

1 CORINTHIANS The letters that are now called 1 and
2 Corinthians actually belong to an original collection of four letters to the Corinthian church. The first of these letters, which is
now lost, is referred to in 1 Corinthians 5:9: "When I wrote to
you before, I told you not to associate with people who indulge
in sexual sin." One topic of this first letter seems to have been a
contribution to be made for Christians in Jerusalem. Shortly after
his first letter, however, Paul received news of various problems
in the Corinthian church, so he sent a second letter, now called
1 Corinthians, to address the issues of concern.

Paul wrote 1 Corinthians from Ephesus (16:8), probably
around the year A.D. 56. His allusion to Passover imagery in
5:7 suggests that he was writing around the time of Passover.

The city of Corinth was well known for its wealth and commerce, which resulted from its ideal location on the Greek peninsula. In Paul's time it was the capital of the the Greek province
of Achaia and the seat of the Roman proconsul. The city was
notorious for wild living—even among jaded Roman soldiers—
so much so that the Greek phrase "to Corinthianize" had become
a proverbial phrase for engaging in sexually immoral behavior.
This climate no doubt contributed to many of the problems in the
Corinthian church.

Several of the problems Paul addresses in 1 Corinthians had
been communicated to him by a Corinthian church member.
There were rival factions, incest among believers, public law-
suits between fellow Christians, abuses of spiritual gifts, and dis-
orderly conduct during church meetings and the Lord's Supper.

Paul addresses each of these problems, pointing to Christ as the ultimate solution.

Paul also answers questions that the Corinthians had asked in a letter (7:1). He counsels them about marriage and sexual relations, about eating food that had been offered to idols, about the use of spiritual gifts in public worship, and about the resurrection of Christ and his followers. In the end, Paul gives them instructions for the collection to be taken for needy Christians in Jerusalem (16:1).

This letter is a prime example of what has been called the *occasional* epistle. That is, while the letter contains a few themes and systematic discourses, it focuses primarily upon specific issues that need to be corrected. First Corinthians provides the Christian church with an actual sample of how specific problems were addressed and corrected in the early church.

Prologue (1:1-9)
Addressing Factions within the Church (1:10–4:21)
Addressing Moral and Ethical Problems (5:1–6:20)
Instruction about Marriage (7:1-40)
Instruction about Questionable Practices (8:1–11:1)
Instruction about Corporate Worship (11:2–14:40)
Instruction about the Resurrection (15:1-58)
Conclusion (16:1-24)

2 CORINTHIANS   The letter now called 2 Corinthians may very well contain both the third and fourth letters that Paul sent to Corinth. Paul makes reference to a third letter in 2 Corinthians 7:8: "I am no longer sorry that I sent that letter to you, though I was sorry for a time, for I know that it was painful to you for a little while." Apparently 1 Corinthians failed to remedy the problems at Corinth, and so did an ensuing visit to the church. The Corinthian church was being troubled by some "false apostles," who were attempting to undermine Paul's authority. In order to defend his apostolic position, Paul wrote the Corinthians a stern letter, which may in fact be 2 Corinthians 10–13.

A little while later, when Paul was in Macedonia, Titus met him with good news from the Corinthian church: The believers had repented of their rebellion and were heeding Paul's instruction. Paul rejoiced at this news and sent yet another letter to the church (A.D. 57). This final letter is now called 2 Corinthians (possibly ending at chapter 9).

Second Corinthians is a very emotional, personal, and autobiographical epistle. Paul freely expresses his emotions, showing both depression and elation over the Corinthian church. Because he regards the Corinthians as his dear children, Paul forgoes formality and politeness, choosing instead to cut to the heart of the issue. He rebukes them sharply for questioning his authority, yet he just as easily praises them for repenting. Paul did not mince words regarding his authority as an apostle—he fiercely defends his commission by recounting his trials for the sake of the gospel. But Paul also reveals the anxiety he suffered while waiting for the church's response to his defense.

Introduction (1:1-11)
The Nature of Paul's Apostolic Ministry (1:12–7:4)
Paul's Reconciliation with the Church (7:5-16)
Collection for the Christians at Jerusalem (8:1–9:15)
Paul's Defense of His Apostolic Authority (10:1–13:10)
Conclusion (13:11-13)

ROMANS Of all the epistles of Paul, the letter to the Romans is the longest, the most elaborate, and the most systematic in design. It is more like a theological treatise than a personal letter, establishing a solid framework for understanding the broad scope of the gospel.

Paul opens his discourse by discussing humanity's relationship to God. Paul describes the human race as violators of holy law, which has been made evident in nature for pagans and in Scripture for Jews. Once Paul establishes humanity's fallenness, he offers a solution—the sacrifice of Jesus Christ. This sacrifice for sin can only be obtained through faith. After a believer receives remission for sin, new life is gained in Jesus Christ. Paul uses several paragraphs to elaborate on each of these points.

Paul then moves into a discussion of Israel's place in God's grand scheme of history. In many respects this section is perhaps the most difficult to fully comprehend, as it sorts out God's purposes for allowing Israel (on the whole) to reject the gospel and allowing the Gentiles to embrace it. Paul discusses the future roles of Israel and the Gentile nations in the kingdom of God.

After this digression Paul returns to his earlier train of thought and discusses the practical application of it. Paul finally concludes this lofty discourse with heartfelt salutations to several believers in Rome.

It is almost certain that Paul wrote this epistle from Corinth in the spring of A.D. 58. At that time he was on his way to Jerusalem to deliver the collection from the Asian churches. After that he hoped to visit Rome on his way to Spain (15:23-28). Given his comments about longing to visit those in Rome (1:13), Paul probably had never yet been to the church in Rome until sometime after he had written to them. The church had apparently been established by other leaders or by those who had become believers during Peter's ministry at Pentecost.

While there was certainly a sizeable Jewish population in Rome at this time, it seems clear that Paul addressed his letter principally to Gentiles (1:13; 15:15-16). But it is equally evident that the church there included Jewish Christians as well, since

Paul bases his entire argument upon principles from the Old Testament. Regardless of the letter's recipients, Paul's epistle to the Roman church provides the Christian church with a fairly systematic understanding of the gospel of Jesus Christ. Paul's framework in Romans has formed the backbone for much of Christian theology today.

> Introduction (1:1-17)
> All Humanity Needs Salvation (1:18–3:20)
> Righteousness by Faith (3:21–5:21)
> New Life in the Spirit (6:1–8:39)
> Israel in the Plan of God (9:1–11:36)
> Living as a Christian (12:1–15:13)
> Conclusion (15:14–16:27)

EPHESIANS   The letter now addressed to the Ephesians was probably originally written as an encyclical—a letter circulated to several churches—for Asia, including Ephesus. This theory is supported by the fairly impersonal and universally applicable subject matter of the letter, despite Paul's three-year stay in Ephesus. There are no personal greetings or specific exhortations, unlike Paul's other letters. Paul addresses his readers as those who have only heard of his ministry (3:2), unlike the Ephesian believers. In addition, the earliest manuscripts of this epistle do not contain the words "in Ephesus" in the opening greeting. It is also possible that this letter is, in fact, the letter to the Laodiceans mentioned at the end of Colossians (4:15-16). Paul instructs the Colossians to trade letters with them, which lends support to the idea that it was written to be circulated among the churches.

Regardless of its intended recipients, the message of Ephesians remains clear: The universal church forms the unified body of Christ. The churches surrounding Ephesus were comprised of both Jewish and Gentile Christians (Acts 19:8-10). It was Paul's great desire to show them that they—as Jews and Greeks—are equal members in the body of Christ. In Christ all believers become one body with equal privileges for all (2:14-22). Paul explained that Jewish and Gentile Christians are comembers of the body and coheirs to God's promises in Christ (3:2-6). Since this epistle is Paul's treatise on the universal church, it is not encumbered with local issues. Instead, it soars above mundane affairs and presents a heavenly view of the church, as it fits into God's eternal plan.

Assuming that Ephesians was written at about the same time as Colossians, Paul probably penned this letter during the early part of his imprisonment in Rome (ca. A.D. 61). A few features of both letters suggest that Ephesians and Colossians were written around the same time. The two letters contain a significant number of parallel passages. Both letters also mention that Tychicus would be coming to visit the recipients.

Paul's presentation of the church reaches its pinnacle in this epistle. Paul depicts the church in ideal perfection, as seen from heaven—but not yet fully manifested on earth. Paul uses a wide variety of images to communicate God's grand conception of the church: It is Christ's body (1:22-23), God's masterpiece (2:10), the household of God (2:19), and the bride of Christ (5:23-32). Paul uses many other images as well. The letter to the Ephesians provides the Christian church with a grand vision of itself toward which it can continually grow.

Introduction (1:1-2)
God's Eternal Purpose for the Church (1:3-23)
The Creation of the Church (2:1-22)
The Mystery Explained (3:1-13)
Paul's Prayer for the Believers (3:14-21)
Unity of the Church (4:1-16)
Living as Children of Light (4:17–5:20)

Right Relationships in the Church (5:21–6:9)
Spiritual Warfare (6:10-20)
Conclusion (6:21-24)

COLOSSIANS   Paul's letter to the Colossians attempts to counter various philosophical influences that had crept into the church there. The text of Colossians suggests that the church had been infiltrated by a syncretistic philosophical system that combined elements of legalistic Judaism, asceticism, and Gnosticism. The Gnostic element was the most pronounced, and Paul gives it the greatest attention.

Colossae was a city in Asia Minor near Ephesus. The church there was composed mainly of Gentiles (2:13). Apparently Paul had never visited the Colossian church, but he had received word about it through Epaphras, who may have founded the church. Epaphras's report prompted Paul to write to the Colossians. This letter was most likely written during Paul's first imprisonment at Rome (A.D. 61). Paul probably also wrote Ephesians around this time, as evidenced by a number of parallel passages with Colossians. The short epistle to Philemon, a member of the Colossian church, was sent along with the letter to the Colossians.

In order to better understand Paul's reasoning in his letter to the Colossians, it is essential to become familiar with Gnosticism. While there were various forms of Gnosticism in Paul's day, a few basic concepts were generally assumed by all of them. All Gnostics believed matter to be inherently evil, which led to a belief in mediating beings between God and creation. If God was truly good, then he could not possibly have anything to do with evil creation. Therefore there must be a series of "aeons," or emanations from God, each a little more distant from him and each having a little less deity. At the end of this chain of intermediate beings there is an emanation possessing enough deity to create a world but removed far enough from

God that his creative activities could not compromise the perfect purity of God. In light of these beliefs, the Christian concept of the Incarnation in Jesus Christ caused a problem for Gnostics. Either Jesus was not fully divine, or else he must have only appeared to be human.

In order to combat this distortion of Jesus Christ's true identity, Paul emphasizes the all-sufficiency and preeminence of Christ. Throughout this short epistle, Paul uses almost thirty different images to describe Christ, including the redeemer (1:14), God's visible image (1:15), the firstborn of all creation (1:15), the head of the body (1:18), the beginning (1:18), the firstborn from the dead (1:18), the preeminent one (1:18), the embodiment of all God's fullness (1:19), the mediator of reconciliation (1:20), the hope of glory (1:27), the mystery of God (2:2), the head of every ruler and authority (2:10), the reality of all shadows (2:16-17), the one hidden in God (3:3), our life (3:4), the one who will appear with us in glory (3:4), and the forgiver (3:13). Paul leaves no questions as to the preeminence of Christ.

The style of this epistle is unique; many Greek phrases occur here that are found nowhere else in the New Testament. Paul's lofty and elaborate discourse corresponds to the majestic nature of his theme—the majesty of Christ's person and office. Paul intentionally uses many phrases belonging to Gnostic philosophy in order to portray Jesus Christ as the answer to the Colossians' questions.

> Introduction (1:1-14)
> The Supremacy of Christ (1:15-23)
> Paul's Labor for the Church (1:24–2:5)
> Dealing with Heresies (2:6-23)
> The New Life versus the Old (3:1–4:6)
> Conclusion (4:7-18)

PHILEMON Paul's brief letter to Philemon, a member of the Colossian church, provides a glimpse into the personal interactions of Paul and other believers. This epistle, probably written on a single leaf of papyrus, makes a personal plea to Philemon to welcome back his runaway slave, Onesimus. Paul even appears to do a bit of subtle arm-twisting to encourage Philemon to forgive Onesimus.

Paul's letter to Philemon is closely linked with his letter to the Colossians. The two epistles include salutations from the same people (except for Justus). Paul mentions in both letters that he is a prisoner. It is also almost certain, therefore, that the letter to Philemon was sent along with the Colossian letter, as Onesimus returned to his owner. This would mean that the letter to Philemon was written from Rome during Paul's imprisonment around A.D. 61.

Apparently Onesimus had run away from Philemon sometime earlier and had become a Christian under Paul's ministry. Onesimus seems to have become an assistant to Paul, until it was decided that he should return to his owner. Paul appeals to Philemon "because of [their] love," although he makes it very clear that he could rightfully order Philemon to receive Onesimus back. He points out that Onesimus is now Philemon's brother in Christ. Paul offers to repay Philemon for anything that Onesimus owes him, while mentioning that Philemon owes Paul his very life. Paul ends the epistle by asking Philemon to prepare a place for him to stay, because Paul expected to be set free from prison soon and planned to visit Colossae.

Greetings (1-3)
Thanksgiving and Prayer (4-7)
Paul's Plea for Onesimus (8-21)
Conclusion (22-25)

PHILIPPIANS Paul's letter to the Philippian believers is perhaps the warmest and most encouraging of all his letters. The object of the epistle is general: Paul wants to thank the Philippians for their contribution to him and to express his love and sympathy for them.

Although some scholars have argued that it was written in Caesarea or Ephesus, Philippians was probably written in Rome near the end of Paul's first imprisonment there (A.D. 62). The reference to "Caesar's palace" (4:22) and to the "palace guard" (1:13) tend to support this location.

Philippi was a leading Macedonian city and a Roman colony. Its inhabitants were transplanted from Rome and were given the full rights of Roman citizenship. They were not subject to the regional government, and they maintained their own senate and magistrates. Paul founded the church there, along with Silas and Timothy (Acts 16:12), and visited it a couple of times throughout his ministry. The church probably consisted mostly of Gentiles, since there were not even enough Jews to form a synagogue when Paul first arrived. Paul's sufferings at Philippi (Acts 16:19) strengthened ties between him and his Philippian converts, who were also exposed to trials for the gospel's sake. They alone sent supplies for Paul's needs on several occasions (Philippians 4:10-18).

As Paul wrote to thank the Philippians for their gift, he opened his letter with details about his condition as a prisoner and about Epaphroditus's condition. Epaphroditus probably held a leading office in the Philippian church, perhaps as an elder. He had become ill for a time and had almost died, but then he recovered. Paul also exhorted the Philippians to imitate Jesus Christ. He used what was probably an early Christian hymn to describe the humility and glorification of Christ (2:6-11).

The second section of the letter cautions the believers against those who want to impose Mosaic law upon them. Paul reveals that he has every reason to boast in his Jewish heritage, but he refuses to do so because it is of little account when compared to the value of knowing Jesus Christ.

In the third section, Paul gently admonishes a few individuals and the church in general, and he thanks them for their gift. In general, it should be said that this epistle reveals Paul's strong desire to know Christ, to be like him, and to glorify him— whether by life or by death. The letter to the Philippians contains no bold censures but focuses instead upon encouraging the church to become like Christ.

> Introduction (1:1-11)
> Paul's Personal Circumstances (1:12-26)
> Living the Christian Life (1:27–2:18)
> Paul's Coworkers, Timothy and Epaphroditus (2:19-30)
> Pursuing the Knowledge of Christ (3:1–4:1)
> Exhortations to Unity, Joy, and Peace (4:2-9)
> Thanks for the Philippians' Gift (4:10-20)
> Conclusion (4:21-23)

The Pastoral Epistles

The epistles known as 1 Timothy, 2 Timothy, and Titus are called the Pastoral Epistles because they are letters of instruction to particular church leaders—namely, Timothy and Titus. Paul's authorship of the Pastoral Epistles is a topic of much debate. Several reasons have been posited against Pauline authorship, but none of them are conclusive. Some have cited that the book of Acts does not include events surrounding the writing of these letters. While this is true, it does not disprove Pauline authorship. Rather, it shows that Paul could have written the Pastoral Epistles after his first imprisonment (which is where the narrative of Acts ends).

Other scholars have noted that the style of the Pastoral Epistles is different from the style of the other Pauline letters. It is evident in Paul's other letters, however, that his style passed through various phases of development. His early epistles are all similar in style and vocabulary, while his later epistles differ from them. Likewise, the Pastoral Epistles resemble each other while differing from the earlier letters. The occasions and conditions for each writing brought forth new expressions to meet the need. In addition, Paul may have used an amanuensis (personal scribe) to help compile the Pastoral Epistles.

The seemingly developed system of church structure has also been given as a case against Pauline authorship. The mere mention of "overseers," however, does not necessarily relegate these letters to the second century. Throughout the Pastoral Epistles, *overseer* seems to be synonymous with *elder*. Likewise in Philippians 1:1, Paul greets the "elders" ("overseers") along with the deacons.

The Pastoral Epistles provide the Christian church with mature insight from the aged apostle to the Gentiles. Paul instructs Timothy and Titus in much the same way as a father teaches his maturing children.

1 TIMOTHY   Paul's first letter to Timothy was written to encourage the young leader to take care of the Ephesian church while Paul was absent. Many scholars believe that 1 Timothy was written sometime between Paul's first and second imprisonment in Rome (ca. A.D. 63). Paul may have been in Corinth at the time he wrote this letter.

In this letter Paul directs Timothy to combat teaching that strays from the apostle's instruction (1:3-20). He gives Timothy instructions for worship in church meetings, for the selection of qualified elders and deacons, and for the appointment of widows to church service. Paul also advises the young church leader regarding how he should relate to older members of the church, as well as to female members. This is followed by a personal appeal to Timothy, as a man of God, to fight the good fight of faith until the time of the Lord's appearing (6:11-16).

> Salutation (1:1-2)
> Warning against False Teachers (1:3-11)
> God's Grace to Paul (1:12-20)
> Instructions on Worship (2:1-15)
> Qualifications for Leaders (3:1-16)
> Instructions to Timothy (4:1-16)
> Advice about Widows, Elders, and Slaves (5:1–6:3)
> False Teachers and Lovers of Money (6:3-10)
> Paul's Final Exhortation (6:11-21)

TITUS   The purpose of Paul's letter to Titus was to instruct Titus in leading the churches on the island of Crete. Titus, a Greek Gentile, was a young coworker of Paul. Paul probably wrote to Titus from Corinth sometime after his first imprisonment (ca. A.D. 65).

During Titus's ministry on Crete, several corrupt elements began to emerge in the churches there. These false teachings were similar to those noticed under Timothy's ministry in Ephesus: Jewish legalism, elements of Gnosticism, and immoral behavior. Paul tried to guide Titus in overcoming these influences. He reiterated the qualifications of elders and explained the virtues that should be displayed among believers. He also directed Titus to encourage the Cretans to adorn the gospel by living industrious, honest lives. The stereotype of Cretans at the time was not very admirable, as evidenced by Paul's quote from the Cretan poet Epimenides. Paul wanted the Cretan church to overcome this dubious reputation and honor God.

Salutation (1:1-4)
Qualifications for Leaders (1:5-9)
Warning against False Teachers (1:10-16)
Right Living in the Church (2:1-15)
Right Living in Society (3:1-11)
Conclusion (3:12-15)

2 TIMOTHY   The final letter of Paul in the New Testament is his second letter to Timothy. Nearing the end of his life, Paul charges Timothy with some final duties as a young leader of the church. As he instructs Timothy to hold fast to the sound teaching of the apostles, Paul, in a sense, is passing on the baton of the Christian faith.

After Paul's release from his first imprisonment in Rome (ca. A.D. 63), Paul wrote to Timothy and Titus from Corinth. At some point Paul visited Troas, where he left some books and a cloak with Carpus (4:13). Eventually Paul returned to Rome, where he was imprisoned a second time, possibly on charges of setting fire to Rome (A.D. 64) or of propagating a novel and unlawful religion in the empire. This imprisonment was much harsher than the first, as 2 Timothy indicates (2:9). From his prison Paul wrote this second letter to Timothy shortly before his execution (ca. A.D. 68). It is not certain where Timothy was at this time. Based on the greetings and references in the letter, it is possible that Timothy was still in Ephesus.

As the time of Paul's execution drew near, he grew anxious to see his disciple, Timothy. Paul asks Timothy to come visit him soon and to bring Mark (another of Paul's coworkers) with him (4:9-13). He also asks Timothy to bring the cloak and books that he left in Troas. Paul seems uncertain, however, that Timothy will arrive in time, and so he shares some final words in his letter. He warns Timothy against heresies that were infecting the churches and encourages him to preach the Scriptures, promoting godly living and spiritual perseverance. He exhorts Timothy to pass on the teachings of the apostles to faithful believers.

As he penned his final words to Timothy, Paul encouraged his young disciple to press on in the faith, as he himself had done. Near the end of his letter, Paul included what could be considered an inspiring epitaph for any believer: "As for me, my life has already been poured out as an offering to God. The time of my death is near. I have fought a good fight, I have finished the race, and I have remained faithful" (4:6-7).

> Salutation (1:1-2)
> Exhortation to Faithfulness (1:3-18)
> A Call to Fervency and Endurance (2:1-13)
> A Workman Approved by God (2:14-26)
> Facing Difficult Times (3:1-17)
> Paul's Final Words (4:1-8)
> Conclusion (4:9-22)

The General Epistles

The New Testament concludes with several books that are called the General Epistles. They are also known as the Catholic (universal) or the Common Epistles. This might be somewhat misleading, however, because some of the General Epistles are addressed to specific readers (1 Peter, 2 John, 3 John). The common characteristic of all of these letters is that they are non-Pauline epistles.

JAMES   The epistle of James to the "twelve tribes in the dispersion" was written like a collection of wise Jewish teachings, much like Jesus' Sermon on the Mount. There are striking similarities in language and style between this epistle and Jesus' Sermon. James even uses the word *synagogue* rather than *church* as the place of meeting for believers (2:2), betraying his Jewish background. Nevertheless, the letter does ground itself as a Christian epistle (1:1; 2:1).

The Jewish tone of this letter lends strong support to the traditional claim that James, the brother of Jesus and elder of the Jerusalem church, was its author. He would certainly be very familiar with Jewish styles of writing, and the Jerusalem church was described in Acts 21:18-24 as taking the law of Moses very seriously. Though James was not one of the original twelve apostles, his close relation to Jesus gave him similar authority, and this is what enabled the epistle to be included in the New Testament canon. The letter's very Jewish tone and its salutation to "the twelve tribes," combined with its complete silence about the Jewish/Gentile controversy, lead many scholars to date this letter very early. It may even have been written as early as A.D. 45.

This letter discusses the gospel in relation to the Law, which the Jews so revered. As Paul's epistles reflect on doctrines emanating from Christ's death and resurrection, so James's epistle focuses on Jesus' teachings. In both the Sermon on the Mount and the epistle of James, true fulfillment of the law flows out of genuine love on the part of the believer. For James, practice, not profession, is the test of true obedience (2:17; 4:17). Likewise, faith without works is seen as dead and useless. James uses the Old Testament figure Abraham as an example of one who was justified not by faith alone but by works, when he offered Isaac as a sacrifice to God (2:20-23). It is interesting to note that Paul used the very same character to prove what appears to be just the opposite point: Abraham was justified because he believed God's promises, not because he had done anything (Romans 3–4).

This apparent tension between James and Paul has caused many Christians difficulty over the centuries. Martin Luther is perhaps the most noted example. He once described James's letter as "an epistle of straw . . . destitute of an evangelical character." Since Luther's time, however, many scholars have argued that James does not oppose the doctrine of justification by faith, as taught by Paul. While looking at justification from distinct standpoints, Paul and James mutually complement each other's definitions. Paul saw faith as producing justification, which in turn produces good works. James saw good works as the genuine proof that one had faith and was therefore justified.

Salutation (1:1)
Trials and Temptations (1:2-18)
Doers of the Word (1:19-27)
Rebuking Favoritism (2:1-13)
Faith and Works (2:14-26)
Controlling the Tongue (3:1-12)
Two Kinds of Wisdom (3:13-18)
Warnings against Worldliness and Wealth (4:1–5:6)
Concluding Exhortations (5:7-20)

HEBREWS   This nameless epistle, later entitled "to the Hebrews," reflects upon the superiority of Christ and the new covenant over Judaism and the old covenant. For some believers, the excitement of Christianity began to wane as time and persecution dragged on, and many considered reverting to Judaism. In order to dissuade them, the author of Hebrews used the Old Testament to show that Jesus Christ has fulfilled and superseded the old covenant of Judaism.

The identity of the author of Hebrews has been anyone's guess over the centuries. The letter does not open with the standard introduction that identifies the author. It is clear, however, that the author was highly fluent in Greek, as evidenced by the myriad of refined phrases and literary devices used throughout the letter. Much of the author's reasoning suggests a penchant for Alexandrian modes of thought. While the actual syntax and phrases of the letter do not resemble Paul's, the general concepts conveyed do resemble the apostle's. This fact, as well as the author's familiarity with Timothy (13:23), suggest that the author was at least a close associate of Paul. These criteria would narrow the field of likely candidates to Apollos, Barnabas, Luke, or possibly even Priscilla. This lack of agreement over the epistle's authorship, however, only serves to emphasize the strength of its content. It is beautifully written, brilliantly structured, and genuinely communicated.

The date of the epistle's composition and the believers to whom it was written are also open to question. Many scholars suspect that it was written to believers in Rome, given the greetings from Christians "from Italy" (13:24). Other scholars posit Alexandria as the destination, since the Muratorian Canon mentions an "epistle to the Alexandrians" in its list. The author's assumption of ongoing priestly practices suggests that the letter was written before the destruction of the temple in A.D. 70.

The epistle to the Hebrews opens by showing that the New Covenant is superior to the old by virtue of Jesus Christ's superiority over the angels and the prophets. Jesus is superior to Moses as well, and yet he was able to identify with humanity, since he became fully human. Jesus is the perfect High Priest, as shown by the Old Testament passages about Melchizedek, the priest to whom Abraham gave a tithe. All this contributes to Jesus' perfect sacrifice for sin, which replaces the sacrifices of the old covenant. If all this is true, then the readers must not fall away from following Christ, but instead they must continue in faith, as did the great heroes of the past. The readers are then given some final warnings and instructions in how to live as Christians in a hostile world.

The letter to the Hebrews provides the church with a brilliant portrayal of the preeminence of Jesus Christ. Yet the book captures the humanity of Jesus just as vividly. Few other New Testament books so artfully and effectively utilize Old Testament concepts to illuminate the significance of Jesus Christ.

> Prologue (1:1-4)
> Jesus Christ, the Superior Messenger (1:5–2:18)
> Jesus Christ, the Superior Apostle (3:1–4:13)
> Jesus Christ, the Superior Priest (4:14–7:28)
> Jesus Christ's Better Covenant (8:1–9:28)
> Jesus Christ's Better Sacrifice (10:1-39)
> Faith, the Better Way (11:1–12:29)
> Conclusion (13:1-25)

1 PETER   This letter was written to Christians who were living as "foreigners" in Asia Minor. These Christians were being persecuted and ostracized by their pagan neighbors. The epistle consoles the persecuted believers and prepares them for even harder times. These sufferings would perfect the believers' faith and purify their souls. The letter also encourages all believers— husbands and wives, masters and slaves, elders and laity—to live godly lives in the presence of unbelievers, thereby giving testimony to Jesus Christ.

Peter identifies himself at the opening of the letter as the author, although he notes that Silvanus actually wrote it down for him. Silvanus's influence accounts for the very refined Greek used in this letter. It is clear that the author, who is a "witness to the sufferings of Christ" (5:1), is the apostle Peter himself. Peter was probably in Rome at the time he wrote this epistle, since "Babylon" (5:13) was the usual Christian code word for "Rome" in the first century. This word is also used in Revelation 14:8 and 16:19 as a code word for Rome. This would fit the strong tradition that Peter ministered primarily in Rome. The fairly developed churches and the persecutions mentioned in the letter suggest a later date for the letter's composition, possibly around A.D. 63.

The regions to which Peter addressed this letter are listed in the order that a messenger would follow to deliver mail in Asia Minor. Most of the churches in these provinces (Pontus, Galatia, Cappadocia, Asia, and Bithynia) were started by Paul and his associates. These churches probably consisted primarily of Jewish Christians, but they also had Gentile Christians as well.

Salutation (1:1-2)
A Holy People for God (1:3–2:12)
Learning to Be Submissive (2:13–3:7)
Suffering as Christians (3:8–5:11)
Conclusion (5:12-14)

2 PETER   The epistle called 2 Peter is markedly different from the first letter attributed to this apostle. This second epistle warns readers against false teachers and encourages them to grow in the knowledge of Jesus Christ.

Peter's authorship of this epistle has been questioned throughout the centuries for several reasons. These reasons include: (1) The epistle was not readily accepted in the early church; (2) the writing style of this epistle is different from 1 Peter; (3) Peter's name has been connected with many Gnostic pseudepigrapha (*The Gospel of Peter, The Acts of Peter, The Teaching of Peter, The Letter of Peter to James, The Preaching of Peter*); and (4) 2 Peter shares some of the same material found in Jude.

Since Silvanus is not mentioned in 2 Peter, he probably did not help write this letter as he did with 1 Peter. This could account for the differences in writing style between the two letters. Perhaps Peter wrote this letter himself. If he did, it was probably between A.D. 66 and 68, just prior to his martyrdom. Peter may have been in Rome at the time he wrote this generically addressed epistle.

One interesting note about this letter is its use of apocalyptic and extrabiblical imagery. It vividly describes demons that are chained in darkness awaiting judgment. The letter closes with a warning to lead lives that anticipate the return of the Lord.

Salutation (1:1-2)
Instructions for Living Godly Lives (1:3-11)
The Authenticity of Peter's Message (1:12-21)
Warning against False Teachers (2:1-22)
The Coming of the Lord (3:1-16)
Conclusion (3:17-18)

JUDE   This short letter was written to counter false teaching that was infecting the early church. The epistle condemns those who reject the authority of the apostles and live self-indulgent, lustful lives.

The author identifies himself as Jude, a brother of James. It is assumed that James is the brother of Jesus, and, therefore, Jude must also be a brother of Jesus. The fact that this letter shares a large amount of material with 2 Peter does not help in dating its composition, since it is not clear which author borrowed from which letter. The letter appears to have been an open letter to the church in general, rather than to any specific church.

This epistle also contains some extrabiblical imagery, and it even quotes from the apocryphal book of *1 Enoch*. Though this letter is one of the shortest in the New Testament, it contains perhaps the most elaborate of all benedictions.

Introduction (1-2)
Warning against False Teachers (3-16)
Standing Firm in the Faith (17-23)
Conclusion (24-25)

1 JOHN   Three letters are traditionally attributed to the apostle John, based upon their linguistic and theological similarities with the Gospel of John. All three letters were probably written at about the same time, possibly before John penned his Gospel (ca. A.D. 85). John may have been in Ephesus as he wrote, since he served as an elder there for many years.

The first letter is very different from the typical epistle format of the first century. It skips the introduction, leaving the letter unsigned and unaddressed. Instead, it starts right into its very concise yet very significant message concerning the person of Jesus Christ.

This first epistle was prompted by a heretical faction that had developed within the church. Apparently this faction had eventually left the church, but seeds of doubt still remained in the minds of many believers (2:18-19). The faction had distorted the apostles' teachings about the person of Christ, denying that Jesus Christ had actually come in the flesh (4:1-3). It is very possible that this heresy was a form of Docetism, which asserted that Christ only "appeared" to come in the flesh.

In order to redirect the believers in the right way, John urges his readers to walk in the light with God and with fellow Christians, to confess their sins, to love God and others, to purify themselves from worldly lusts, to follow the Spirit of truth in discerning false teachings, and to esteem Jesus Christ as the true God. John stresses the importance of fellowship in order to safeguard against further factions and heresies in the future.

> Prologue (1:1-4)
> Fellowship with the Father and the Son (1:5–2:29)
> Love among God's People (3:1–4:21)
> True Faith (5:1-12)
> Conclusion (5:13-21)

2 JOHN   This brief second letter of the apostle John contains much of the same language and thoughts of the first letter. In typical letter format, 2 John opens by identifying "the Elder" (John) as its author and addressing itself to "the chosen lady and to her children." The corporate tone of the letter suggests that "the chosen lady" refers to a church rather than an actual woman.

> Salutation (1-3)
> Encouragement and Warnings (4-11)
> Conclusion (12-13)

3 JOHN   The third letter of John ("the Elder") was written to Gaius. Although the New Testament mentions several men with the name Gaius, it would be difficult to say which, if any, of these was the recipient of this epistle. In any event, John penned this short letter to give notice of his upcoming visit to the church in Gaius's locality. A certain man named Diotrephes had taken control of the church and was refusing to receive John or anyone sent by him. Diotrephes even expelled people from the church who accepted anyone sent there by John. John warns the believers that he will deal with Diotrephes when he arrives. John commends Demetrius for his upright Christian life.

> Salutation (1-2)
> Commending Gaius (3-8)
> Condemning Diotrephes (9-10)
> Commending Demetrius (11-12)
> Conclusion (13-15)

THE GOSPELS AND ACTS

The life and ministry of Jesus Christ forms the core of the Christian faith, so it is important for believers to learn about him. During the first several decades following Jesus' death and resurrection, the oral traditions of the apostles were the most reliable sources for learning about Jesus. The New Testament books repeatedly note the importance of the apostles' ministry as they worked to accurately inform the church about Jesus Christ. All teachings about Jesus had to conform to the apostles' oral accounts.

As time wore on, however, the apostles grew older and some passed away, leaving fewer and fewer sources for reliable information about Jesus. The solution was to write down the apostles' teachings in order to preserve their authoritative message for later generations. These written accounts came to be known as "Gospels."

Opinions differ about whether or not the gospel was a new literary form in the first century. Some scholars argue that the gospel as a literary form has no real parallel outside of the New Testament writings and should not be compared with concurrent Jewish or Greek literature. Others insist that the gospel resembles other biographies or hero stories of Greek and Jewish literature.

While it is true that the Gospels are unique in many respects, especially regarding their assertion that Jesus is the Messiah, they do seem to contain some features of other ancient biographies. It would be only natural for a first-century writer to present a collection of oral traditions about Jesus in a form that readers would recognize and understand. Gentile readers, familiar with biographies of great men, likely would have understood the Gospels as such. Likewise, Jewish readers probably would have associated the Gospels with the familiar hero narratives of the Old Testament, for the Gospels are, indeed, hero stories on a grand scale. They are an excellent example of narrative built on the life of an exemplary protagonist whose acts and words are treasured and celebrated.

It is important to recognize, however, that the Gospel writers truly did believe in the content of their narratives. They were not merely spinning yarns about a fictitious legend. They believed that Jesus really is the Messiah, and their stories were written to communicate this all-important message.

MARK   The Gospel according to Mark is probably the earliest of the existing Gospels. Matthew and Luke probably used Mark as a source for their Gospels, which would account for the large amount of verbatim parallels among them. These three accounts are commonly called the synoptic Gospels.

The title of this Gospel, "according to Mark," almost certainly refers to John Mark of Acts 12:25. He was the nephew of Barnabas, an early Jewish Christian in the church at Jerusalem. The Roman name "Mark" was perhaps a badge of Roman citizenship, as in Paul's case, or it may have been adopted when he left Jerusalem to serve the Gentile church in Antioch. Mark has a history of affiliation with the apostle Peter. When an angel of the Lord freed Peter from prison, the apostle went directly to "the home of Mary, the mother of John Mark" (Acts 12:12). Peter also mentions in his first letter that his "son" Mark was with him in "Babylon" (5:13), a code name for Rome. Tradition holds that Mark ministered in Rome with Peter in his later years and compiled his Gospel from Peter's teachings about Jesus Christ (ca. A.D. 63). This tradition is further supported by the Gospel's tendency to focus on Peter's words and deeds (8:29-33; 9:4-7; 10:28-31; 14:29-31, 66-72), and even on Peter himself (16:7).

Several features about this Gospel suggest that it was written for Gentile believers in Rome. Mark is careful to explain Jewish customs (7:3-4; 14:12; 15:42), to translate Aramaic expressions into Greek (3:17; 5:41; 7:11, 34; 15:22, 34), to use Latin terms and measurements (5:9; 6:27, 48; 12:15, 42; 13:35; 15:16, 39), and to record a profession of faith from a Roman centurion at the cross (15:39).

Since Mark's audience was composed primarily of believers, who should have already been familiar with the major events of Jesus' life, he did not attempt to write an exhaustive biography. Rather, Mark used an abbreviated account of the life and works of Jesus to present him as the Messiah and to provide the church with a dynamic model of Christian life and service—especially in the face of intense opposition.

The Gospel of Mark opens with the preaching of John the Baptist and the baptism of Jesus. Almost immediately after this event, Jesus begins performing miracles and preaching about the kingdom of God. Jesus is constantly on the move throughout the narrative, and his teaching is interspersed throughout his miracles. Mark notes that Jesus taught mostly in parables. Mark seems to regard Jesus' actions, however, as of greatest significance.

Throughout the book, the Son of God, the Messiah, is constantly presented as very much human. Likewise, Jesus constantly points to God rather than to himself, further emphasizing his humanity. Halfway through the book Jesus finally reveals his identity as the Messiah, but he warns his disciples that he must go to Jerusalem to be crucified. He is hailed as king upon entering Jerusalem, but then he is killed one week later.

The Gospel closes with the story of Jesus' resurrection, but it appears to have been left incomplete (according to the most reliable manuscripts). The story ends as the women leave the empty tomb in fear and tell no one. It is possible that the last pages of the Gospel were lost very soon after they were written.

At the time this Gospel was written (ca. A.D. 63), the Christians in Rome were living under the reign of Nero, who despised Christianity. Many Christians were being persecuted and even killed for their faith. The Gospel of Mark would have greatly encouraged the Roman believers, since it describes how Jesus labored in the face of constant opposition and resolutely determined to fulfill his destiny on the cross. Mark's Gospel also develops a theology about Jesus as God's Son and as humanity's servant, but the primary purpose of the Gospel was to preserve a record of the life and actions of Jesus the Messiah.

Opening Events of Jesus' Ministry (1:1-13)
Jesus' Early Galilean Ministry (1:14–3:6)
Second Phase of Galilean Ministry (3:7–7:23)
Third Phase of Galilean Ministry (7:24–9:50)
Jesus' Journey to Jerusalem (10:1-52)
Jesus' Final Week in Jerusalem (11:1–15:47)
Jesus' Resurrection (16:1-8)
The Longer Ending of Mark (16:9-20)

MATTHEW   Though it is clear that the Gospel of Matthew includes a significant amount of material from the Gospel of Mark, it is difficult to determine just when the Gospel was compiled. There is even debate over which Gospel came first. The early church recognized Matthew as the first Gospel and placed it first in the New Testament canon. The genealogy that introduces this Gospel also provided a convenient segue from the Old Testament to the New Testament. Many scholars today, however, place the date of Matthew's composition after Mark, possibly around A.D. 65.

The early church fathers recognized the apostle Matthew as the author of this Gospel. The title "according to Matthew" could have been added later, so it is difficult to be certain if Matthew was indeed the author. Since there is little evidence that significantly calls this into question, however, there is little reason to question the tradition that the educated tax collector is the author of this Gospel.

Assuming that Matthew was written after Mark, it appears that the author used Mark as a framework for the life and actions of Jesus and expanded upon it with additional information and sayings of Jesus. Many scholars argue that Matthew, as well as Luke, made use of a collection of Aramaic sayings of Jesus as he compiled his Gospel in Greek. While this is possible, it is still debated. Nevertheless, it is clear that Matthew placed a great deal of emphasis on Jesus' parables and teachings, as well as his deeds.

Matthew's Gospel has been described as the Gospel written for the Jews. Its Jewish focus and flavor are evident throughout the book. Matthew contains more than fifty Old Testament quotations and more than seventy-five other allusions. Matthew opens his Gospel by tracing Jesus' descent from Abraham and David. Matthew uses Jewish terminology and does not bother to explain Jewish customs. To do so was unnecessary because his readers were predominantly Jewish. Another Jewish theme in this Gospel is Jesus' image as the Messiah who fulfills the Old Testament prophecies.

While it is fairly certain, then, that Matthew wrote this Gospel to convince Jews that Jesus is the Messiah and that he has ushered in the kingdom of heaven, it is also clear that Matthew wanted to emphasize the Gentiles' inclusion in the kingdom. Jesus is presented as God's servant sent to the Gentiles (12:18-21), and the apostles are sent by Jesus to make disciples of all the nations (28:19). The kingdom of heaven would be filled with Jews and Gentiles alike through the work of Jesus Christ.

According to Matthew's presentation, the kingdom of heaven arrived on earth with the birth of Jesus Christ, and it would continue to be revealed in various phases. The advent of Jesus marked the first manifestation of the kingdom. To believe in Jesus as the Messiah granted the believer entrance into the kingdom. The final arrival of the kingdom was postponed by the

Jews' rejection of Jesus (21:42-43). Much of Jesus' language concerning the kingdom indicates a future reign. In the meantime, the kingdom will be coexistent with the church (16:18-19) and will reside in people's hearts (13:3-23). Eventually the kingdom of heaven will be displayed in full power and glory on the earth after Jesus Christ has returned.

> Jesus' Birth and Infancy (1:1–2:23)
> The Beginning of Jesus' Ministry (3:1–4:25)
> The Sermon on the Mount (5:1–7:29)
> Jesus' Miracles (8:1–9:34)
> Jesus Sends Out the Twelve Disciples (9:35–10:42)
> The Claims of Jesus (11:1–12:50)
> Parables of the Kingdom of Heaven (13:1-52)
> Jesus Rejected and John the Baptist Beheaded
>   (13:53–14:12)
> Jesus Leaves Herod's Dominion (14:13–17:27)
> Jesus' Teachings on Forgiveness (18:1-35)
> Jesus' Journey to Jerusalem (19:1–20:34)
> Jesus' Final Week in Jerusalem (21:1–28:10)
> Events Following the Resurrection (28:11-20)

LUKE   The Gospel of Luke and the book of Acts were written as a two-part sequel sometime between A.D. 60 and 70. Acts was written shortly after Paul's two-year imprisonment (ca. A.D. 60–62) mentioned in Acts 28:30.

The preface to the Gospel indicates that Luke was not an eyewitness or immediate disciple of Jesus; he received his information from others who had been with Jesus. Luke carried out extensive research and then wrote an orderly account about Jesus.

This Gospel, as well as the book of Acts, traditionally has been ascribed to Luke the physician. Although he is not mentioned by name in either of these books, Luke is the most reasonable candidate for authorship. He was an associate of Paul throughout his ministry to the Gentiles. Luke himself was a Gentile and would have been fluent in Greek. This would account for the highly refined grammar and vocabulary of Luke and Acts. The similarities in content between the Gospel of Luke and Paul's writings lend further support to Luke's authorship. Luke's account of the Last Supper is exactly the same as Paul's (cf. Luke 22:19-20 with 1 Corinthians 11:23-25). When Paul mentions the post-Resurrection appearances, he recalls that Jesus was first seen by Peter and then by the Twelve (1 Corinthians 15:4-5). Luke alone among the Gospel writers affirms that Jesus appeared first to Peter and then to the Twelve (Luke 24:34).

Since Paul was the apostle to the Gentiles, it is no surprise that his associate, Luke, would write a Gospel for the Gentiles—specifically for a Gentile convert named Theophilus. Luke penned an account to verify the facts of Jesus' life and ministry and, in so doing, to establish and fortify Theophilus's faith. Of course Luke's readership would extend beyond Theophilus to many readers with many needs, but this Gospel was initially aimed to help Gentile converts become grounded in their newfound faith. Like Matthew, Luke appears to have used Mark as a framework for his Gospel, and he, too, includes material that may have come from a collection of Aramaic teachings of Jesus.

When the Gospel of Luke is compared to the other Gospels, certain emphases become apparent. These features become even more apparent when Luke's sequel, the book of Acts, is taken into account. Luke was keenly interested in the inclusion of the whole world in the gospel of Jesus Christ. Many of Jesus' parables reflect this concern for Gentiles as well as Jews. Luke also focuses upon individual believers, social outcasts, women, children, and the poor. Luke highlights prayer and the work of the

Holy Spirit, and this results in a striking note of joyfulness and praise throughout his Gospel.

Jesus' Background and Early Life (1:1–2:52)
The Ministry of John the Baptist (3:1-20)
The Beginning of Jesus' Ministry (3:21–4:13)
Jesus' Ministry in Galilee (4:14–9:50)
Jesus' Journey to Jerusalem (9:51–19:44)
Jesus' Final Week in Jerusalem (19:45–23:56)
Jesus' Resurrection and Appearances (24:1-53)

ACTS The book of Acts, in addition to the third Gospel, was written by Luke shortly after Paul's first imprisonment in Rome (ca. A.D. 60–62). Originally Luke and Acts were written as a two-volume work for a believer named Theophilus (Acts 1:1-3). During the second century, the Gospel of Luke was separated from Acts when it was added to the three other Gospels to form a single collection. It is important to remember, however, that the two books were written as a single work and therefore complement each other.

As in the Gospel of Luke, the language of Acts resembles refined classical Greek mingled with Semitic phrases from time to time. Luke includes himself at several places throughout the narrative, as is noted by his use of "we" in reference to Paul's entourage (16:10-17; 20:5-15; 21:1-18; 27:1–28:16).

The book of Acts is basically a synopsis of early church history. The book divides itself into six sections by inserting a verse after each section that makes a positive statement concerning the spread of the gospel and the church.

The book of Acts (sometimes called "the Acts of the Apostles") begins with the outpouring of the promised Holy Spirit at Pentecost. The apostles (formerly called disciples) immediately begin proclaiming the gospel of Jesus Christ and performing miracles through the Holy Spirit. The apostles begin their activities in Jerusalem, expand to Asia Minor and Europe, and eventually reach Rome, covering most of the Roman Empire over time. The first half of the book focuses on the work of Peter and the other apostles. The second half follows Paul on his missionary journeys, giving a general overview of the growth of the early church. The gospel is first presented only to Jews, and some receive it. Others reject it, and this precipitates Paul's move to minister primarily among the Gentiles. The church dramatically expands among the Gentiles. A critical point in the narrative is the Jerusalem Council, which was formed in order to resolve the debate over the role of Mosaic law among Gentile Christians. After the council decides not to impose the entire Mosaic law upon Gentile believers, the church expands even more. Along the way, Paul is continually plagued by persecution, by danger, and by Jews who are zealous to uphold Mosaic law.

> The Church in Jerusalem (1:1–6:7)
> The Church throughout Palestine (6:8–9:31)
> The Church in Antioch (9:32–12:24)
> The Church throughout Asia Minor (12:25–16:5)
> The Church throughout Europe (16:6–19:20)
> The Church at Rome (19:21–28:31)

JOHN The Gospel of John was the last of the four Gospels to be written. It is markedly different from the three synoptic Gospels in several ways. The basic plot structure does not follow the book of Mark. For example, Jesus travels to Jerusalem several times throughout the Gospel of John, unlike the synoptic accounts, where a single trip to Jerusalem provides the climax of the story. John's account also focuses predominantly on Jesus' teaching and the theological significance of his life and actions.

Several theological and stylistic similarities have convinced many scholars that the author of this Gospel is the same one who wrote the epistles of John. While the writer is not specifically named in the Gospel, he gives every indication that he is indeed John, "the disciple whom Jesus loved." This apostle was one of the three disciples (along with Peter and James, John's brother) who were especially close to Jesus. John is thought to have ministered at Ephesus until the reign of Trajan (ca. A.D. 98). The final composition of John's Gospel—including the epilogue (chapter 21)—could have taken place anywhere between 80 and 100 A.D. It could be that the initial work began even earlier, and then the final draft, complete with the appended epilogue, was finished later.

The Gospel of John was written fairly late in New Testament history, so its contents reveal different emphases from those of the synoptic Gospels. John was much more interested in explaining who Jesus *is* than what he did. This is made immediately evident by the prologue to the Gospel, which describes Jesus Christ as "the Word" who is God and who has been with God since the beginning of time (1:1). Furthermore, he is the unique Son of God, who is able to reveal the Father to humans (1:18). Throughout the rest of the book, Jesus carries out this role as he interacts with his disciples and argues with his opponents. Jesus' miracles are referred to as "signs" of greater truths, rather than as mere displays of divine power. The stories recounted by John are filled with symbolic and theological meaning, such as Jesus' repeated use of the phrase "I am" (4:26; 8:24; 13:19). This is the same name that God used for himself when he spoke to Moses in the Old Testament.

John wrote his Gospel to convince readers that "Jesus is the Messiah, the Son of God, and that by believing in him you will have life" (20:31). He made a special effort to encourage those who had come to believe in Jesus Christ, despite never having seen him (20:29). John's Gospel is probably the most universally appealing book in the New Testament. It brilliantly conveys developed theology through warmly intimate interactions and discussions with Jesus Christ.

The Prologue (1:1-18)
Jesus' First Disciples (1:19-51)
Jesus' Public Ministry: Seven Signs (2:1–12:51)
Jesus' Discourse in the Upper Room (13:1–17:26)
Jesus' Arrest, Trial, and Crucifixion (18:1–19:37)
Jesus' Burial and Resurrection (19:38–20:31)
The Epilogue (21:1-25)

. . . . .REVELATION

The Revelation (or "Apocalypse") of John is undoubtedly the most difficult and confusing book for most readers of the New Testament. The book is a combination of both epistle and apocalyptic prophecy. The first three chapters are written as letters to seven churches in Asia Minor. The rest of the book recounts a fantastic vision involving bizarre creatures, divine beings, symbolic signs and numbers, and various plagues and curses. At the end of this extraordinary vision, the faithful are rewarded, and the evil are condemned.

The author of this book is traditionally held to be the apostle John. The book itself identifies its author as John (1:1, 4, 9; 22:8) but does not specify which one. The earliest church writers state that John was exiled to Patmos under the emperor Domitian (ca. A.D. 90–95). It is here that John recorded his symbolic visions for the churches of Asia Minor. For many scholars, however, the content and style of Revelation seem so radically different from John's other writings that they find it difficult to believe these books were all written by the same author. Even the early church was divided over this issue. The Eastern church questioned John's authorship for centuries and so were slow to include Revelation in the canon. The Western church was less apprehensive and added the book to the canon much earlier.

Regardless of the author's identity, the purpose of the book remains clear: to encourage and exhort Christians who were undergoing persecution for their faith. By the time Revelation was being written, the church had been subjected to fierce persecution under both Nero and Domitian. Christians were harassed, evicted, tortured, and killed for believing in Jesus Christ, much like the Jews who were persecuted by the Seleucids and Antiochus Epiphanes centuries earlier. In order to give hope to these believers, John recorded his vision of ultimate redemption for the faithful.

The book of Revelation is replete with what has been termed "apocalyptic" imagery. Apocalypticism grew out of the Seleucid era when, as mentioned earlier, faithful Jews were persecuted for their religious beliefs. In reaction to this persecution, many came to view the world as being temporarily under the reign of the evil one. Ultimately, however, God would supernaturally enter history and restore everything. In the meantime, terrible ordeals and conflicts would occur as portents of the coming end. Many literary works were written from this perspective, and they tended to have similar literary features. These included vision stories, exotic creatures, divine beings, symbolic names and numbers, and cosmic conflicts between good and evil forces. Many extrabiblical works were written as apocalypses (meaning "uncoverings").

Revelation opens with a brief introduction, identifying the book as a prophecy given to John from Jesus Christ. Seven letters to seven churches in Asia Minor follow, citing various shortcomings and giving instruction and correction for their spiritual well-being. It is possible that the seven churches represent the entire church, rather than just the particular ones named, since the number seven was thought to represent completeness or wholeness. These seven letters establish several themes that are addressed later in the apocalyptic narrative section. This connects the body of the book with its beginning, giving a literary unity to the whole work.

The narrative then picks up with another sequence of apocalyptic visions intended to show John "what must happen after these things" (4:1). The imagery portrayed in these visions draws heavily from Old Testament prophecy and from apocalyptic writings such as 2 Esdras and 1 Enoch.

This section opens by ushering the reader into the throne room of God. In God's right hand is a seven-sealed scroll, which the Lamb, Jesus Christ, comes forward to open. As each of the seven seals are broken, various symbolic creatures and events are released. Then the angels of heaven blow seven trumpets, and the same sort of cycle takes place. After this, seven signs are given to represent different events and people. Seven bowls are poured out, unleashing terrible plagues and curses upon the earth. After all this, the fall of "Babylon" is recited, as well as the destruction of a terrible beast and a false prophet. Jesus Christ then returns to the earth to reign for a thousand years. After this era, Satan is released in order to rally his forces for a cataclysmic final battle with the forces of heaven. Satan is finally defeated, and those who sided with him are judged. God finally restores everything by creating a new heaven and a new earth. Revelation then draws to a close where the Old Testament opened—with a perfect world where the tree of life is watered by the freely flowing river of life. The vision ends with Jesus alerting the churches that he is indeed coming soon to fulfill all these things.

This fantastic book is almost certainly the most widely disputed as to its ultimate meaning. There seem to be as many interpretations of its symbolism as there are scholars to study it.

Basically, however, there are three general schools of thought:
(1) Almost the entire prophecy of Revelation refers to events of
the first century; (2) the prophecies delineate the history of the
church from John's time to the end of the world; and (3) almost
the entire prophecy refers to future events to be fulfilled immediately before Christ's second coming. Whatever view is taken, the
presentation in the book itself is that the seven seals, trumpets,
and bowls usher in Christ's return to the earth. At that time
Christ will restore all things and reward the righteous. This reas-
suring thought for persecuted Christians is vividly communicated through the rich imagery of apocalyptic story. The book of
Revelation provides a fitting end to the story of the New Testament.

> Prologue (1:1-8)
> Jesus among the Seven Churches (1:9-20)
> The Letters to the Seven Churches (2:1–3:22)
> The Throne, the Scroll, and the Lamb (4:1–5:14)
> The Seven Seals (6:1–8:1)
> The Seven Trumpets (8:2–11:19)
> The Seven Signs (12:1–14:20)
> The Seven Bowls (15:1–16:21)
> The Destruction of Babylon (17:1–19:10)
> The Destruction of the Beast and False Prophet (19:11-21)
> The Thousand Years (20:1-6)
> Satan's Judgment (20:7-10)
> Great White Throne Judgment (20:11-15)
> New Heaven, New Earth, New Jerusalem (21:1–22:5)
> Epilogue (22:6-21)

SELECTED BIBLIOGRAPHY

The Pentateuch

Alter, Robert. *The Art of Biblical Narrative.* New York: Basic Books, 1983.

Cassuto, U. *Commentary on the Book of Exodus.* Translated by Israel Abrahams. Jerusalem: Magnes Press, 1967.

Clines, D. *The Theme of the Pentateuch.* Sheffield: Almond Press, 1978.

Craigie, P. C. *The Book of Deuteronomy.* New International Commentary on the Old Testament. Grand Rapids: Eerdmans, 1976.

Harrison, R. K. *Leviticus: An Introduction and Commentary.* Tyndale Old Testament Commentaries. Downers Grove, Ill.: InterVarsity Press, 1980.

Hoffmeier, James K. *Israel in Egypt: The Evidence for the Authenticity of the Exodus Tradition.* New York: Oxford University Press, 1997.

Kikiwada, Isaac, and Arthur Quinn. *Before Abraham Was.* Nashville: Abingdon, 1985.

Kitchen, K. *The Bible and Its World.* Downers Grove, Ill.: InterVarsity Press, 1977.

Mann, Thomas W. *The Book of the Torah: The Narrative Integrity of the Pentateuch.* Atlanta: John Knox Press, 1988.

Mayes, A. D. H. *Deuteronomy.* The New Century Bible Commentary. Grand Rapids: Eerdmans, 1979.

Millard, A. R., and D. J. Wiseman. *Essays on the Patriarchal Narratives.* Winona Lake, Ind.: Eisenbrauns, 1983.

Rendsburg, Gary A. *Redaction of Genesis.* Winona Lake, Ind.: Eisenbrauns, 1986.

Snaith, N. H. *Leviticus and Numbers.* The Century Bible. London: Thomas Nelson, 1967.

Speiser, E. A. *Genesis.* The Anchor Bible. Garden City, N.Y.: Doubleday, 1964.

Van Seter, John. *Abraham in History and Tradition.* New Haven: Yale University Press, 1975.

Wenham, Gordon J. *Genesis 1–15.* Word Biblical Commentary. Waco: Word, 1987.

―――. *Genesis 16–50.* Word Biblical Commentary. Waco: Word, n.d.

―――. *The Book of Leviticus.* New International Commentary on the Old Testament. Grand Rapids: Eerdmans, 1979.

―――. *Numbers: An Introduction and Commentary.* Tyndale Old Testament Commentaries. Downers Grove, Ill.: InterVarsity Press, 1981.

Whybray, R. N. *The Making of the Pentateuch: A Methodological Study.* Sheffield: Almond Press, 1987.

History

Baldwin, Joyce. G. *Esther: An Introduction and Commentary.* Tyndale Old Testament Commentaries. Downers Grove, Ill.: InterVarsity Press, 1984.

————. *First and Second Samuel: An Introduction and Commentary.* Tyndale Old Testament Commentaries. Downers Grove, Ill.: InterVarsity Press, 1988.

Butler, Trent. *Joshua.* Word Biblical Commentary. Waco: Word, 1983.

Clines, D. J. *Ezra, Nehemiah, Esther.* The New Century Bible Commentary. Grand Rapids: Eerdmans, 1984.

Cundall, Arthur E., and Leon Morris. *Judges and Ruth.* Downers Grove, Ill.: InterVarsity Press, 1968.

Fensham, F. Charles. *The Books of Ezra, Nehemiah.* New International Commentary on the Old Testament. Grand Rapids: Eerdmans, 1982.

Hayes, J. H., and P. K. Hooker. *A New Chronology for the Kings of Israel and Judah and Its Implications for Biblical History and Literature.* Atlanta: John Knox, 1988.

Huey, F. B. "Esther." In *The Expositor's Bible Commentary.* Vol. 4. Edited by F. E. Gaebelein. Grand Rapids: Zondervan, 1988.

Mazar, Amihai. *Archaeology of the Land of the Bible: 10,000–586 B.C.E.* New York: Doubleday, 1992.

McCarter, P. K. *First Samuel.* The Anchor Bible. Garden City, N.Y.: Doubleday, 1984.

Millard, A. R., et al. eds. *Faith, Tradition, and History: Old Testament Historiography in Its Near Eastern Context.* Winona Lake, Ind.: Eisenbrauns, 1993.

Thiele, Edwin R. *The Mysterious Numbers of the Hebrew Kings.* Grand Rapids: Zondervan, 1984.

Williamson, H. G. M. *Ezra, Nehemiah.* Word Biblical Commentary. Waco: Word, 1985.

Woudstra, M. H. *The Book of Joshua.* New International Commentary on the Old Testament. Grand Rapids: Eerdmans, 1981.

Yamauchi, Edwin M. "Ezra, Nehemiah." In *The Expositor's Bible Commentary.* Vol 4. Edited by F. E. Gaebelein. Grand Rapids: Zondervan, 1988.

Wisdom and Poetry

Andersen, F. I. *Job: An Introduction and Commentary.* Tyndale Old Testament Commentaries. Downers Grove, Ill.: InterVarsity Press, 1976.

Bullock, C. Hassell. *An Introduction to the Old Testament Poetic Books.* Rev. ed. Chicago: Moody Press, 1988.

Crenshaw, James. *Old Testament Wisdom: An Introduction*. Atlanta: John Knox, 1981.

Dhorme, E. A. *A Commentary on the Book of Job*. Nashville: Thomas Nelson, 1984.

Gammie, John G., and Leo G. Perdue, eds. *The Sage in Israel and the Ancient Near East*. Winona Lake, Ind.: Eisenbrauns, 1990.

Gordis, Robert. *The Book of God and Man: A Study of Job*. Chicago: The University Press, 1965.

––––––. *Koheleth: The Man and His World*. New York: Schocken, 1968.

––––––. *The Song of Songs and Lamentations: A Commentary and Translation*. New York: Ktav Publishing, 1974.

Scott, R. B., ed. *Proverbs and Ecclesiastes*. The Anchor Bible. Garden City, N.Y.: Doubleday, 1965.

The Prophets

Allen, L. C. *The Books of Joel, Obadiah, Jonah and Micah*. The New International Commentary on the Old Testament. Grand Rapids: Eerdmans, 1976.

Andersen, F. I., and D. N. Freedman, eds. *Hosea*. The Anchor Bible. Garden City, N.Y.: Doubleday, 1980.

––––––. *Amos: A New Translation*. The Anchor Bible. Garden City, N.Y.: Doubleday, 1989.

Baldwin, Joyce G. *Daniel: An Introduction and Commentary*. Tyndale Old Testament Commentaries. Downers Grove, Ill.: InterVarsity Press, 1978.

––––––. *Haggai, Zechariah, Malachi: An Introduction and Commentary*. Tyndale Old Testament Commentaries. Downers Grove, Ill.: InterVarsity Press, 1972.

Bright, John. *Jeremiah*. The Anchor Bible. Garden City, N.Y.: Doubleday, 1965.

Brownlee, W. H. *Ezekiel 1–19*. Word Biblical Commentary. Waco: Word, 1986.

Bullock, C. Hassell. *An Introduction to the Old Testament Prophetic Books*. Chicago: Moody Press, 1986.

Gaebelein, F. E., ed. "Daniel and the Minor Prophets." *The Expositor's Bible Commentary*. Grand Rapids: Zondervan, 1985.

Hayes, John H., and Stuart A. Irvine. *Isaiah*. Nashville: Abingdon, 1987.

Holladay, W. L. *Jeremiah*. 2 vols. Hermeneia: A Critical and Historical Commentary on the Bible. Philadelphia: Fortress, 1986.

King, Philip J. *Amos, Hosea, Micah: An Archaeological Commentary*. Philadelphia: Westminster, 1988.

Sasson, J. M. *Jonah: A New Translation with Introduction, Commentary, and Interpretation*. The Anchor Bible. Garden City, N.Y.: Doubleday, 1990.

Smith, Ralph L. *Micah—Malachi*. Word Biblical Commentary. Waco: Word, 1984.

Stuart, Douglas. *Hosea—Jonah*. Word Biblical Commentary. Waco: Word, 1989.

Taylor, J. B. *Ezekiel: An Introduction and Commentary*. Tyndale Old Testament Commentaries. Downers Grove, Ill.: InterVarsity Press, 1969.

Thompson, J. A. *The Book of Jeremiah*. New International Commentary on the Old Testament. Grand Rapids: Eerdmans, 1980.

Watts, J. D. W. *Isaiah 1–33*. Word Biblical Commentary. Waco: Word, 1985.

———. *Isaiah 34–66*. Word Biblical Commentary. Waco: Word, 1987.

Wevers, J. W. *Ezekiel*. The New Century Bible Commentary. Grand Rapids: Eerdmans, 1969.

Wiseman, D. J. *Nebuchadnezzar and Babylon*. Oxford: Oxford University Press, 1986.

———. *Notes on Some Problems in the Book of Daniel*. London: Tyndale Press, 1970.

Wolff, Hans W. *Joel and Amos*. Hermeneia: A Critical and Historical Commentary on the Bible. Philadelphia: Fortress, 1977.

The Synoptic Gospels

Aune, David E. *The New Testament in Its Literary Environment*. Vol. 8, Library of Early Christianity. Philadelphia: Westminster 1987.

Caird, George B. *The Gospel of Saint Luke*. Westminster Pelican Series. Philadelphia: The Westminster Press, 1964.

Carson, D. A. "Matthew." In *The Expositor's Bible Commentary*. Vol. 8. Edited by F. E. Gaebelein. Grand Rapids: Zondervan, 1984.

Cole, A. *The Gospel according to Mark*. Tyndale New Testament Commentary. Grand Rapids: Eerdmans, 1961.

Conzelmann, Hans. *The Theology of Saint Luke*. New York: Harper & Row, 1960.

Cranfield, C. E. B. *The Gospel according to Saint Mark*. Cambridge: Cambridge University Press, 1959.

Ellison, H. L. "Matthew." In *The New Layman's Bible Commentary*. Glasgow: Pickering & Inglis, 1979.

Geldenhuys, Johannes. *Commentary on the Gospel of Luke*. New International Commentary. Grand Rapids: Eerdmans, 1951.

Hunter, A. M. "The Gospel according to Saint Mark." In *Torch Bible Commentary*. London: SCM, 1967.

Liefeld, Walter. "Luke." In *The Expositor's Bible Commentary*. Vol. 8. Edited by F. E. Gaebelein. Grand Rapids: Zondervan, 1984.

Lightfoot, Neil. *Parables of Jesus*. Grand Rapids: Baker Book House, 1963.

Manson, T. W. *The Sayings of Jesus*. London: SCM, 1949.

Marshall, I. Howard. *Luke: Historian and Theologian.* Grand Rapids: Zondervan, 1971.

Nineham, D. E. *Studies in the Gospels.* Naperville, Ill.: Allenson, 1955.

Nixon, R. E. "Matthew." In *The New Bible Commentary: Revised.* London: InterVarsity Press, 1970.

Schweizer, Eduard. *The Good News according to Mark.* London: SPCK, 1971.

Taylor, Vincent. *The Gospel according to Saint Mark.* London: Macmillan, 1952.

Tinsley, E. J. *Gospel according to Luke.* Cambridge Bible Commentary on the New English Bible. Cambridge: Cambridge University Press, 1965.

Walvoord, John. *Matthew: Thy Kingdom Come.* Chicago: Moody, 1974.

Wessel, Walter. "Mark." In *The Expositor's Bible Commentary.* Vol 8. Edited by F. E. Gaebelein. Grand Rapids: Zondervan, 1978.

John

Barrett, C. K. *The Gospel according to Saint John.* Philadelphia: The Westminster Press, 1978.

Bruce, F. F. *The Gospel of John.* Grand Rapids: Eerdmans, 1982.

Dods, Marcus. "The Gospel of Saint John." In *The Expositor's Greek Testament.* London: Hodder and Stoughton, 1899.

Moberly, R. C. *Atonement and Personality.* London: John Murray, 1909.

Morris, Leon. *The Gospel according to John.* Grand Rapids: Eerdmans, 1971.

Pink, A. W. *Exposition of the Gospel of John.* Grand Rapids: Zondervan, 1973.

Titus, Eric L. *The Message of the Fourth Gospel.* Nashville: Abingdon Press, 1967.

Westcott, B. F. *The Gospel according to Saint John.* 1881. Reprint, Grand Rapids: Zondervan, 1973.

Acts

Bruce, F. F. *The Acts of the Apostles.* Chicago: InterVarsity Press, 1952.

Conybeare, W. J., and J. S. Howson. *The Life and Epistles of Saint Paul.* 1851. Reprint, Grand Rapids: Eerdmans, 1978.

Longenecker, Richard. "The Acts of the Apostles." In *The Expositor's Bible Commentary.* Vol. 9. Edited by F. E. Gaebelein. Grand Rapids: Zondervan, 1981.

Metzger, Bruce M. *The New Testament: Its Background, Growth, and Content.* 2nd ed. Nashville: Abingdon Press, 1965, 1983.

The Letters of Paul to the Churches

Barrett, C. K. *A Commentary on the Epistle to the Romans.* New York: Harper & Brothers, 1957.

Berkhof, Hendrikus. *Doctrine of the Holy Spirit*. Atlanta: John Knox Press, 1976.

Boice, James M. "Galatians." In *The Expositor's Bible Commentary*. Vol. 10. Edited by F. E. Gaebelein. Grand Rapids: Zondervan, 1978.

Bruce, F. F. *The Epistle of Paul to the Romans*. In the Tyndale New Testament Commentaries. Grand Rapids: Eerdmans, 1963.

————. "The Epistle to the Colossians, to Philemon, and to the Ephesians." In *The New International Commentary on the New Testament*. Grand Rapids: Eerdmans, 1984.

Brunner, Emil. *The Letter to the Romans, A Commentary*. London: Lutterworth, 1959.

Constable, Thomas L. "First Thessalonians." In *The Bible Knowledge Commentary*. Wheaton, Ill.: Victor Books, 1983.

Davidson, F., and Ralph Martin. "Romans." In *The New Bible Commentary: Revised*. Edited by Guthrie and Motyer. London: InterVarsity Press, 1953, 1970.

Fee, Gordon. "The First Epistle to the Corinthians." In *The New International Commentary on the New Testament*. Grand Rapids: Eerdmans, 1987.

Gaffin, Richard. *The Centrality of the Resurrection*. Grand Rapids: Baker Book House, 1978.

Harris, Murray J. "Second Corinthians." In *The Expositor's Bible Commentary*. Vol. 10. Edited by F. E. Gaebelein. Grand Rapids: Zondervan, 1978.

Hawthorne, Gerald. *Philippians*. Vol. 43, Word Biblical Commentary. Waco: Word, 1983.

Hillyer, Norman. "First and Second Corinthians." In *The New Bible Commentary: Revised*. London: InterVarsity Press, 1970.

Kent, Homer. "Philippians." In *The Expositor's Bible Commentary*. Vol. 11. Edited by F. E. Gaebelein. Grand Rapids: Eerdmans, 1978.

Lightfoot, J. B. *The Epistle of Saint Paul to the Galatians*. 1865. Reprint, Grand Rapids: Zondervan, 1957.

————. *Saint Paul's Epistles to the Colossians and to Philemon*. New York: Macmillan & Co., 1879.

————. *Saint Paul's Epistle to the Philippians*. New York: Macmillan & Co., 1868.

————. *Saint Paul's Epistle to the Romans*. London: Macmillan & Co. 1913.

Lightner, Robert. "Philippians." In *The Bible Knowledge Commentary*. Wheaton, Ill.: Victor Books, 1983.

Lincoln, Andrew T. *Ephesians*. Vol. 43, Word Biblical Commentary. Waco: Word, 1990.

Luther, Martin. *Commentary on the Epistle to the Romans.* 1522. Reprint, Grand Rapids: Zondervan, 1954.

————. *A Commentary on Saint Paul's Epistle to the Galatians.* 1535. Reprint, Westwood, N.J.: Fleming H. Revell, 1953.

Mare, W. Harold. "First Corinthians." In *The Expositor's Bible Commentary.* Vol 10. Edited by F. E. Gaebelein. Grand Rapids: Zondervan, 1978.

Meeks, Wayne. *The First Urban Christians: The Social World of the Apostle Paul.* New Haven, Conn: Yale University Press, 1984.

Rupprecht, Arthur A. "Philemon." In *The Expositor's Bible Commentary.* Vol. 11. Edited by F. E. Gaebelein. Grand Rapids: Zondervan, 1978.

Thomas, Robert L. "First Thessalonians." In *The Expositor's Bible Commentary.* Vol. 11. Edited by F. E. Gaebelein. Grand Rapids: Zondervan, 1978.

————. "Second Thessalonians." In *The Expositor's Bible Commentary.* Vol. 11. Edited by F. E. Gaebelein. Grand Rapids: Zondervan, 1978.

Vaughn, Curtis. "Colossians." In *The Expositor's Bible Commentary.* Vol. 11. Edited by F. E. Gaebelein. Grand Rapids: Zondervan, 1978.

The Pastoral Epistles

Calvin, John. *Commentaries on the Epistles to Timothy, Titus, and Philemon.* 1856. Reprint, Grand Rapids: Eerdmans, 1948.

Earle, Ralph. "First Timothy." In *The Expositor's Bible Commentary.* Vol. 11. Edited by F. E. Gaebelein. Grand Rapids: Zondervan, 1978.

————. "Second Timothy." In *The Expositor's Bible Commentary.* Vol. 11. Edited by F. E. Gaebelein. Grand Rapids: Zondervan, 1978.

White, Newport J. D. "First and Second Epistles to Timothy." In *The Expositor's Greek Testament.* Grand Rapids: Eerdmans, 1979.

The General Epistles

Bauckham, Richard J. *Jude, 2 Peter.* Vol. 50, Word Biblical Commentary. Waco: Word, 1983.

Blum, Edwin A. "Jude." In *The Expositor's Bible Commentary.* Vol. 12. Edited by F. E. Gaebelein. Grand Rapids: Zondervan, 1981.

————. "First Peter." in *The Expositor's Bible Commentary.* Vol. 12. Edited by F. E. Gaebelein. Grand Rapids: Zondervan, 1981.

————. "Second Peter." In *The Expositor's Bible Commentary.* Vol. 12. Edited by F. E. Gaebelein. Grand Rapids: Zondervan, 1981.

Bruce, F. F. *The Epistles of John: Introduction, Exposition, Notes.* Grand Rapids: Eerdmans, 1970.

Burdick, Donald W. "James." In *The Expositor's Bible Commentary.* Vol. 12. Edited by F. E. Gaebelein. Grand Rapids: Zondervan, 1981.

Calvin, John. *The Epistles of Paul the Apostle to the Hebrews and the First and Second Epistles of Saint Peter.* Edinburgh: Oliver & Boyd, 1963.

Hawthorne, Gerald F. "The Letter to the Hebrews." In *Bible Commentary for Today.* Glasgow: Pickering & Inglis, 1979.

Kelly, J. N. D. *A Commentary on the Epistles of Peter and Jude.* The Harper New Testament Commentaries. New York: Harper & Row, 1969.

Marshall, I. H. "The Epistles of John." In *The New International Commentary.* Grand Rapids: Eerdmans, 1978.

Mayor, J. B. "The Epistle of Jude." In *The Expositor's Greek Testament.* Grand Rapids: Eerdmans, 1979.

Morris, Leon. "Hebrews." In *The Expositor's Bible Commentary.* Vol. 12. Edited by F. E. Gaebelein. Grand Rapids: Zondervan, 1981.

Smith, David. "First John." In *The Expositor's Greek Testament.* Grand Rapids: Eerdmans, 1979.

Vine, W. E. *The Epistles of John: Light, Love, Life.* Grand Rapids: Zondervan, 1970 (by permission of Oliphants).

Westcott, B. F. *The Epistle to the Hebrews.* London: Macmillan & Co., 1892.

Revelation

Beasley-Murray, G. R. "The Revelation." In *The New Bible Commentary: Revised.* Grand Rapids: Eerdmans, 1970.

Bruce, F. F. "The Revelation to John." In *A New Testament Commentary.* Grand Rapids: Zondervan, 1969.

Bullinger, E. W. *Commentary on Revelation.* 1935. Reprint, Grand Rapids: Kregel, 1984.

Caird, G. B. *The Revelation of Saint John the Divine.* The Harper New Testament Commentaries. New York: Harper & Row, 1966.

Hendriksen, William. *More than Conquerors; an Interpretation of the Book of Revelation.* Grand Rapids: Baker Book House, 1967.

Johnson, Alan F. "Revelation." In *The Expositor's Bible Commentary.* Vol. 12. Edited by F. E. Gaebelein. Grand Rapids: Zondervan, 1981.

Ladd, George E. *A Commentary on the Revelation of John.* Grand Rapids: Eerdmans, 1972.

McDowell, Edward A. *The Meaning and Message of the Book of Revelation.* Nashville: Broadman Press, 1951.

Seiss, Joseph A. *Apocalypse.* Grand Rapids: Zondervan, n.d.

Swete, Henry Barclay. *The Apocalypse of Saint John.* New York: Macmillan & Co., 1906.

Torrance, Thomas F. *Apocalypse Today.* Greenwood, S.C.: Attic Press, 1960.

Trench, Richard C. *Commentary on the Epistle to the Seven Churches.* Reprint, Minneapolis: Klock & Klock, 1978.

Walvoord, John F. *The Revelation of Jesus Christ.* Chicago: Moody Press, 1966.